The Collected Works Of Padraic H. Pearse:
Plays, Stories, Poems

Padraic Pearse

Printing Statement:

Due to the very old age and scarcity of this book,
many of the pages may be hard to read due to the
blurring of the original text, possible missing pages,
missing text, dark backgrounds and other issues
beyond our control.

Because this is such an important and rare work, we
believe it is best to reproduce this book regardless of
its original condition.

Thank you for your understanding.

PUBLISHER'S NOTE

This volume of the Collected Works of Padraic
Pearse contains his English Versions of Plays and
Poems, many of which have not been previously
published. The Author's final copies of the
manuscripts of THE SINGER and THE MASTER
were burnt in the Publisher's office at Easter,
1916, but, fortunately, other copies of these
manuscripts, apparently containing the Author's
corrections, were forthcoming. On page 35 of THE
SINGER, there was one page of manuscript missing
which evidently contained dialogue covering the
exit of MacDara and the entrance of Diarmaid,
and it seemed better to leave a blank here than
to have the missing speeches written by another
hand. Towards the end of this play there were
some pages of manuscript giving a slightly
different version, and it was difficult to say
whether this version was an earlier or later one
than the manuscript which has been followed.
This fragment has been printed as an Appendix.

The Translations of the Stories from the Irish
were made by Mr. Joseph Campbell.

In the Author's Manuscript, the play THE
SINGER was dedicated "To My Mother."

The Publisher wishes to thank *An Clodhanna
Teoranta* for the permission accorded to Mrs.
Pearse to publish translations of *Iosagan*, *An
Sagart*, *Bairbre*, *Eogainin na nEan*.

INTRODUCTION

It must be evident to all who read this collection of plays, stories and poems in the spirit which their author would have wished for, that it would be utterly wrong to preface them with remarks applying merely to their literary qualities.

For they are something more than literature. On the pages as we read they seem to grow into flesh and blood and spirit. They are a record of the emotions of a life which was devoured by one idea, the native beauty of Ireland, its manners, its speech, its people, its history. And we see how that idea was coupled in the mind with a poignant sense of the danger that threatened the vitality of all those things. The writer saw the thought of the Gall spreading like a destructive growth through the body of Irish nationality. He felt that an imported politeness mocked at the Gaelic ways; he knew that the Irish language had been extinguished in the greater part of Ireland by the sense of shame working on poverty,

and that many of the people of the Irish-
speaking fringe were also growing ashamed
of the priceless treasure they possessed ; he
saw that the lessons of Irish history, which
the leaders of the past had taught by their
labours and often sealed with their blood,
were being ignored in the modern political
game.

Earnestness of purpose had always marked
him. He threw his heart and soul and
strength into the Gaelic movement ; he
learned the language so thoroughly as to
be able to use it with ease as his medium
of literary expression, to recapture the old
forms of poetry and story-telling, and to
infuse into them the modernity of his own
modes of thought. He fought the battles
of Irish with a vigour that we all remember.
He founded a school—against what diffi-
culties !—where education was Irish, and
aimed at the free development of personality
in the Irish way. All that was hard and
earnest work, but its earnestness was nothing
to the terrible seriousness that grew upon
him when he came to realize the maladies
of the political movement that was supposed
to aim at Irish nationhood. The Volunteers,

INTRODUCTION

at whose foundation he had assisted, were at
first negotiated with and then divided by the
constitutional Party ; the original founders,
who determined to adhere to their principles,
were left high and dry without any constitutional support.   The conviction gained on
him that only blood could vivify what tame-
ness and corruption had weakened, and that
he and his comrades were destined to go
down the same dark road by which so many
brave and illustrious Irishmen had gone
before them.

It is in the light of this progress of
thought that we must read his writings.
We find the fresh notes of tenderness and
sweetness in the early stories, Iosagan, The
Priest, Barbara, and Eoineen of the Birds.
The psychology of children, their sorrows
and joys, are the theme.   The older people
are merely foils to the children ; we learn
nothing of their inner story, except in the
case of Old Matthias—and even here we
have merely an account of a return to the
innocence of second childhood.   Iosagan
coming to play with the little ones on the
green, while the old folks are at Sunday
Mass, Paraic wearing a surplice and saying

INTRODUCTION

Dominus Vobiscum, and *Orate Fratres*, in anticipation of the priestly office, Brideen holding converse grave and gay with her doll, Eoineen watching with joy the return of the swallows in spring, and broken-hearted at their departure in late autumn, all pass before our eyes as dwellers in a *Tír-ná-n-óg* in *Iar-Connacht*, where the waves sing a careless song, and the sun shines only on innocent faces. But in THE MOTHER and other stories we are on different ground, and are told of " the heavy and the weary weight " that lies on the hearts of the Western poor. We see the tragic pride of Gaelic culture that impels old Brigid of the Songs to walk across Ireland to sing at the Oireachtas in Dublin, only to die of hunger and exhaustion at the end, the listless face of the old tramp, who tells how through the Dearg-Daol he had lost his luck, his farm and his family, and had become " a walking man, and the roads of Connacht before him, from that day to this "; and even more significant is the story of the death in prison of Coilin, with its under-current of hatred for the foreign laws. The manner of narration in these stories is brief

and severe ; there is scarcely a phrase too
many, and even purists would be hard set
to detect an alien note. The most perfect
instance seems to me to be the story of the
DEARG-DAOL.

Of the little collection of poems, *Suan-
traighe agus Goltraidhe* (Songs of Sleep and
Sorrow), Mr. MacDonagh rightly said:
"One need not ask if it be worth while
having books of such poetry. The production of this is already a success for the
new literature." The old forms, with their
full-sounding assonances and alliterations
are beautifully wrought, and the modern
thoughts, the latter-day enthusiasms and
dejections, when they come, never strike us
as intruders. To illustrate their beauty,
quotation in English would not serve my
purpose ; I will quote from the Irish
original a single verse from the poem,
A Chinn Aluinn :

A ghlóir ionmhuin dob'íseal aoibhinn,
An fíor gó gcualas trém'shuanaibh thú ?
Nó an fíor an t-eólas atá dom'bheo-ghoin ?
Mo bhrón, sa tuamba níl fuaim ná guth!

Quite suddenly, in the second last of the

collection, the image of Ireland stands out, bowed beneath the weight of the ages, the mother of Cuchulainn the valiant, but also of shameful children who betrayed her, lonely and imperious. And the last poem is an exquisite farewell to the beauty that is seen and heard and felt, before gathering the pack and going the stern way whither the service of Ireland pointed.

The plays, THE SINGER, THE KING, THE MASTER, and the last poems, THE REBEL, THE FOOL, THE MOTHER, are those of a man in whom meditation on coming struggle, agony and death have become one with life and art. They are weighted with the concept of a nation inheriting an original sin of slavery, for whose salvation the death of one man is a necessity. "One man can free a nation as one Man redeemed the world," says MacDara in THE SINGER. "I will take no pike, I will go into the battle with bare hands, I will stand up before the Gall as Christ hung naked before men on the tree!" And the mother says: "My son, MacDara, is the Singer that has quickened the dead years and all the quiet dust." And the

sharp anguish of doubt is there too, the
ever-recurring thought of the apathy of the
nation, and the vision of those " that cursed
me in their hearts for having brought death
into their houses," of "the wise, sad faces of
the dead, and the keening of women." But
the doubt comes from outside, it is not born
within the soul, and the stern resolution and
saeva indignatio conquer it and persist. The
mother is evoked in whose calendar of saints
the martyrs will be inscribed, who will
ponder at night in her heart in religious
quiet on "the little names that were familiar
once round her dead hearth." And through
all, as if nature would have her revenge
for the over-strain, breaks in a flash the
love of the old-sought, fugitive beauty of
things, the

" Little rabbits in a field at evening
Lit by a slanting sun,
Or some green hill where shadows drifted by,
Some quiet hill where mountainy man hath
    sown
And soon would reap ; near to the gate of
    Heaven ;
Or children with bare feet upon the sands

INTRODUCTION

Of some ebbed sea, or playing on the streets
Of little towns in Connacht."

Taken in the order I have indicated, the
work of Padraic Pearse seems to me to
constitute a mystical book of the love of
Ireland. In *Iosagán* we have the tender
and satisfied love of the fervent novice,
delighting in the old-world, yet ever youth-
ful charm of the Gaelic race, untroubled by
the clouded day of maturity. We find in
An Mátair, and in some of the poems
and plays the way of purgation by doubt
and suffering. In the last plays and poems
we reach unity and illumination, the glow
of the soul in the fire of martyrdom. And
all these states of love are interwoven, as
they should be, in the separate stages, though
a different one may have predominance in
each. I believe the generations of Irishmen
yet to be born into the national faith will
come to the reading of this book as to a kind
of *Itinerarium Mentis ad Deum*, a journey to
the realization of Ireland, past, present and
to come, a learning of all the love and
enthusiasm and resolve which that realization implies:

INTRODUCTION

" Live in these conquering leaves ; live all
    the same ;
And walk through all tongues one triumph-
    ant flame.
Live here, great heart ; and love, and die,
    and kill ;
And bleed and wound ; and yield and con-
    quer still."

Those who look in these pages for a
vision of Pagan Ireland, with its pre-
Christian gods and heroes, will be disap-
pointed. The old divinities and figures
of the sagas are there, and the remnants of
the old worship in the minds of the people
are delineated, but everything is over-
shadowed by the Christian concept, and
the religion that is found here centres in
Christ and Mary. The effect of fifteen
centuries of Christianity is not ignored or
despised. The ideas of sacrifice and atone-
ment, of the blood of martyrs that makes
fruitful the seed of the faith, are to be found
all through these writings ; nay, they have
here even more than their religious signifi-
cance, and become vitalizing factors in the
struggle for Irish nationality. The doubts

and weaknesses which are described are not
those of people who are inclined to return
to the former beliefs, but of men whose
souls are grown faint on account of the
lethargy which they see around them. For
years they have preached and laboured and
sung ; but the masses remain unmoved.
What wonder if they feel unable to repeat
with conviction : " Think you not that I
can ask the Father, and He will give me
presently twelve legions of angels ? "

No, the Ireland about which Pearse writes
is not the land of the early heroes, but of
people deeply imbued with the Christian
idea and will. And yet we feel that the
ancient and mediæval and modern Gaelic
currents meet in him. By his life and death
he has become one with Cuchulainn and
Fionn and Oisin, with the early teachers,
terrible or gentle, of Christianity, with
Hugh of Dungannon and Owen Roe and
all the chieftains who fought against the
growing power of the Sassenach, with
Wolfe Tone and the United Irishmen, with
Rossa, O'Leary, and the Fenians. He will
appeal to the imagination of times to come
more than any of the rebels of the last

INTRODUCTION

hundred and thirty years, because in him all
the tendencies of Irish thought, culture and
nationality were more fully developed. His
name and deeds will be taught by mothers
to their children long before the time when
they will be learned in school histories. To
older people he will be a watchword in the
national fight, a symbol of the unbroken
continuity and permanence of the Gaelic
tradition. And they will think of him forever in different ways, as a poet who sang
the songs of his country, as a soldier who
died for it, as a martyr who bore witness
with his blood to the truth of his faith, as
a hero, a second Cuchulainn, who battled
with a divine frenzy to stem the waves of
the invading tide.

P. BROWNE.

Maynooth, 21st May, 1917.

THE SINGER

*The wide, clean kitchen of a country house.
To the left a door, which when open, shows a
wild country with a background of lonely
hills; to the right a fireplace, beside which
another door leads to a room. A candle
burns on the table.*

*Maire ni Fhiannachta, a sad, grey-haired
woman, is spinning wool near the fire. Sighle,
a young girl, crouches in the ingle nook,
carding. She is bare-footed.*

MAIRE. Mend the fire, Sighle, jewel.
SIGHLE. Are you cold?
MAIRE. The feet of me are cold.

*Sighle rises and mends the fire, putting on
more turf; then she sits down again and
resumes her carding.*

SIGHLE. You had a right to go to bed.
MAIRE. I couldn't have slept, child. I
had a feeling that something was drawing
near to us. That something or somebody
was coming here. All day yesterday I
heard footsteps abroad on the street.

SIGHLE. 'Twas the dry leaves. The quicken trees in the gap were losing their leaves in the high wind.

MAIRE. Maybe so. Did you think that Colm looked anxious in himself last night when he was going out?

SIGHLE. I may as well quench that candle. The dawn has whitened.

She rises and quenches the candle; then resumes her place.

MAIRE. Did you think, daughter, that Colm looked anxious and sorrowful in himself when he was going out?

SIGHLE. I did.

MAIRE. Was he saying anything to you?

SIGHLE. He was. (*They work silently for a few minutes; then Sighle stops and speaks.*) Maire ni Fhiannachta, I think I ought to tell you what your son said to me. I have been going over and over it in my mind all the long hours of the night. It is not right for the two of us to be sitting at this fire with a secret like that coming between us. Will I tell you what Colm said to me?

MAIRE. You may tell me if you like, Sighle girl.

4

SIGHLE. He said to me that he was very fond of me.

MAIRE (*who has stopped spinning*). Yes, daughter?

SIGHLE. And . . . and he asked me if he came safe out of the trouble, would I marry him.

MAIRE. What did you say to him?

SIGHLE. I told him that I could not give him any answer.

MAIRE. Did he ask you why you could not give him an answer?

SIGHLE. He did; and I didn't know what to tell him.

MAIRE. Can you tell me?

SIGHLE. Do you remember the day I first came to your house, Maire?

MAIRE. I do well.

SIGHLE. Do you remember how lonely I was?

MAIRE. I do, you creature. Didn't I cry myself when the priest brought you in to me? And you caught hold of my skirt and wouldn't let it go, but cried till I thought your heart would break. "They've put my mammie in the ground," you kept saying. "She was asleep, and they put her in the ground."

5

SIGHLE. And you went down on your knees beside me and put your two arms around me, and put your cheek against my cheek and said nothing but "God comfort you; God comfort you." And when I stopped crying a little, you brought me over to the fire. Your two sons were at the fire, Maire. Colm was in the ingle where I am now; MacDara was sitting where you are. MacDara stooped down and lifted me on to his knee—I was only a weeshy child. He stroked my hair. Then he began singing a little song to me, a little song that had sad words in it, but that had joy in the heart of it, and in the beat of it; and the words and the music grew very caressing and soothing like, . . . like my mother's hand when it was on my cheek, or my mother's kiss on my mouth when I'd be half asleep —

MAIRE. Yes, daughter?

SIGHLE. And it soothed me, and soothed me; and I began to think that I was at home again, and I fell asleep in MacDara's arms —oh, the strong, strong arms of him, with his soft voice soothing me—when I woke up long after that I was still in his arms

with my head on his shoulder. I opened
my eyes and looked up at him. He smiled
at me and said, "That was a good, long
sleep." I . . . put up my face to him
to be kissed, and he bent down his head
and kissed me. He was so gentle, so
gentle. (*Maire cries silently.*) I had no right
to tell you all this. God forgive me for
bringing those tears to you, Maire ni
Fhiannachta.

MAIRE. Whist, girl. You had a right
to tell me. Go on, jewel . . . my
boy, my poor boy !

SIGHLE. I was only a weeshy child —

MAIRE. Eight years you were, no more,
the day the priest brought you into the house.

SIGHLE. How old was MacDara ?

MAIRE. He was turned fifteen. Fifteen
he was on St. MacDara's day, the year
your mother died.

SIGHLE. This house was as dear to me
nearly as my mother's house from that day.
You were good to me, Maire ni Fhiannachta,
and your two boys were good to me, but—

MAIRE. Yes, daughter ?

SIGHLE. MacDara was like sun and moon
to me, like dew and rain to me, like strength

7

face used to come between me and the white Host.

MAIRE. We have both been lonely for him. The house has been lonely for him.

SIGHLE. Colm never knew I was so fond of MacDara. When MacDara went away Colm was kinder to me than ever,—but, indeed, he was always kind.

MAIRE. Colm is a kind boy.

SIGHLE. It was not till yesterday he told me he was fond of me; I never thought it, I liked him well, but I never thought there would be word of marriage between us. I don't think he would have spoken if it was not for the trouble coming. He says it will be soon now.

MAIRE. It will be very soon.

SIGHLE. I shiver when I think of them all going out to fight. They will go out laughing: I see them with their cheeks flushed and their red lips apart. And then they will lie very still on the hillside,—so still and white, with no red in their cheeks, but maybe a red wound in their white breasts, or on their white foreheads. Colm's hair will be dabbled with blood.

MAIRE. Whist, daughter. That is no

talk for one that was reared in this house. I am his mother, and I do not grudge him.

SIGHLE. Forgive me, you have known more sorrow than I, and I think only of my own sorrow. (*She rises and kisses Maire.*) I am proud other times to think of so many young men, young men with straight, strong limbs, and smooth, white flesh, going out into great peril because a voice has called to them to right the wrong of the people. Oh, I would like to see the man that has set their hearts on fire with the breath of his voice! They say that he is very young. They say that he is one of ourselves,—a mountainy man that speaks our speech, and has known hunger and sorrow.

MAIRE. The strength and the sweetness he has come, maybe, out of his sorrow.

SIGHLE. I heard Diarmaid of the Bridge say that he was at the fair of Uachtar Ard yesterday. There were hundreds in the streets striving to see him.

MAIRE. I wonder would he be coming here into Cois-Fhairrge, or is it into the Joyce country he would go? I don't know but it's his coming I felt all day yesterday,

10

and all night. I thought, maybe, it might
be —

SIGHLE. Who did you think it might be?

MAIRE. I thought it might be my son
was coming to me.

SIGHLE. Is it MacDara?

MAIRE. Yes, MacDara.

SIGHLE. Do you think would he come
back to be with the boys in the trouble?

MAIRE. He would.

SIGHLE. Would he be left back now?

MAIRE. Who would let or stay him and
he homing like a homing bird? Death
only; God between us and harm!

SIGHLE. Amen.

MAIRE. There is Colm in to us.

SIGHLE (*looking out of the window*). Aye,
he's on the street.

MAIRE. Poor Colm !

*The door opens and Colm comes in. He
is a lad of twenty.*

COLM. Did you not go to bed, mother?

MAIRE. I did not, Colm. I was too
uneasy to sleep. Sighle kept me company
all night.

COLM. It's a pity of the two of you to be
up like this.

11

MAIRE. We would be more lonesome in bed than here chatting. Had you many boys at the drill to-night?

COLM. We had, then. There were ten and three score.

MAIRE. When will the trouble be, Colm?

COLM. It will be to-morrow, or after to-morrow; or maybe sooner. There's a man expected from Galway with the word.

MAIRE. Is it the mountains you'll take to, or to march to Uachtar Ard or to Galway?

COLM. It's to march we'll do, I'm thinking. Diarmaid of the Bridge and Cuimin Eanna and the master will be into us shortly. We have some plans to make and the master wants to write some orders.

MAIRE. Is it you will be their captain?

COLM. It is, unless a better man comes in my place.

MAIRE. What better man would come?

COLM. There is talk of the Singer coming. He was at the fair of Uachtar Ard yesterday.

MAIRE. Let you put on the kettle, Sighle, and ready the room. The master will be asking a cup of tea. Will you lie down for an hour, Colm?

Colm. I will not. They will be in on us now.

Maire. Let you make haste, Sighle. Ready the room. Here, give me the kettle.

Sighle, who has brought a kettle full of water, gives it to Maire, who hangs it over the fire; Sighle goes into the room.

Colm (*after a pause*). Was Sighle talking to you, mother?

Maire. She was, son.

Colm. What did she say?

Maire. She told me what you said to her last night. You must be patient, Colm. Don't press her to give you an answer too soon. She has strange thoughts in her heart, and strange memories.

Colm. What memories has she?

Maire. Many a woman has memories.

Colm. Sighle has no memories but of this house and of her mother. What is she but a child?

Maire. And what are you but a child? Can't you have patience? Children have memories, but the memories sometimes die. Sighle's memories have not died yet.

13

MAOILSHEACHLAINN. 'Tis a pity of the women of the world. Too good they are for us, and too full of care. I'm afraid that there was many a woman on this mountain that sat up last night. Aye, and many a woman in Ireland. 'Tis women that keep all the great vigils.

MAIRE (*wetting the tea*). Why wouldn't we sit up to have a cup of tea ready for you? Won't you go west into the room?

MAOILSHEACHLAINN. We'd as lief drink it here beside the fire.

MAIRE. Sighle is readying the room. You'll want the table to write on, maybe.

MAOILSHEACHLAINN. We'll go west so.

MAIRE. Wait till Sighle has the table laid. The tea will be drawn in a minute.

COLM (*to Maoilsheachlainn*). Was there any word of the messenger at the forge, master?

MAOILSHEACHLAINN. There was not.

CUIMIN. When we were coming up the boreen I saw a man breasting Cnoc an Teachta that I thought might be him.

MAOILSHEACHLAINN. I don't think it was him. He was walking slowly, and sure the messenger that brings that great story will come on the wings of the wind.

15

COLM. Perhaps it was one of the boys you saw going home from the drill.

CUIMIN. No, it was a stranger. He looked like a mountainy man that would be coming from a distance. He might be someone that was at the fair of Uachtar Ard yesterday, and that stayed the evening after selling.

MAOILSHEACHLAINN. Aye, there did a lot stay, I'm told, talking about the word that's expected.

CUIMIN. The Singer was there, I believe. Diarmaid of the Bridge said that he spoke to them all at the fair, and that there did a lot stay in the town after the fair thinking he'd speak to them again. They say he has the talk of an angel.

MAOILSHEACHLAINN. What sort is he to look at?

CUIMIN. A poor man of the mountains. Young they say he is, and pale like a man that lived in cities, but with the dress and the speech of a mountainy man; shy in himself and very silent, till he stands up to talk to the people. And then he has the voice of a silver trumpet, and words so beautiful that they make the people cry.

16

And there is terrible anger in him, for all that he is shrinking and gentle. Diarmaid said that in the Joyce country they think it is some great hero that has come back again to lead the people against the Gall, or maybe an angel, or the Son of Mary Himself that has come down on the earth.

MAOILSHEACHLAINN (*looking towards the door*). There's a footstep abroad.

MAIRE (*who has been sitting very straight in her chair listening intently*). That is my son's step.

COLM. Sure, amn't I here, mother?

MAIRE. That is MacDara's step.

All start and look first towards Maire, then towards the door, the latch of which has been touched.

MAOILSHEACHLAINN. I wish it was Mac-Dara, Maire. 'Tis maybe Diarmaid or the mountainy man we saw on the road.

MAIRE. It is not Diarmaid. It is Mac-Dara.

The door opens slowly and MacDara, a young man of perhaps twenty-five, dressed like a man of the mountains, stands on the threshold.

MacDara. God save all here.

All. And you, likewise.

Maire (*who has risen and is stretching out her hands*). I felt you coming to me, little son!

MacDara (*springing to her and folding her in his arms*). Little mother! little mother!

While they still embrace Sighle re-enters from the room and stands still on the threshold looking at MacDara.

Maire (*raising her head*). Along all the quiet roads and across all the rough mountains, and through all the crowded towns, I felt you drawing near to me.

MacDara. Oh, the long years, the long years!

Maire. I am crying for pride at the sight of you. Neighbours, neighbours, this is MacDara, the first child that I bore to my husband.

MacDara (*kissing Colm*). My little brother! (*To Cuimin*), Cuimin Eanna! (*To Maoilsheachlainn*), Master! (*They shake hands.*)

Maoilsheachlainn. Welcome home.

Cuimin. Welcome home.

MacDara (*looking round*). Where is . .
(*He sees Sighle in the doorway.*) Sighle!
(*He approaches her and takes her hand.*)
Little, little Sighle! . . . I . . .
Mother, sometimes when I was in the
middle of great crowds, I have seen this
fireplace, and you standing with your
hands stretched out to me as you stood a
minute ago, and Sighle in the doorway of
the room; and my heart has cried out to
you.

MAIRE. I used to hear the crying of your
heart. Often and often here by the fireside
or abroad on the street I would stand and
say, " MacDara is crying out to me now.
The heart in him is yearning." And this
while back I felt you draw near, draw near,
step by step. Last night I felt you very
near to me. Do you remember me saying,
Sighle, that I felt someone coming, and that
I thought maybe it might be MacDara?

SIGHLE. You did.

MAIRE. I knew that something glorious
was coming to the mountain with to-day's
dawn. Red dawns and white dawns I have
seen on the hills, but none like this dawn.
Come in, jewel, and sit down awhile in the

room. Sighle has the table laid. The tea is drawn. Bring in the griddle-cakes, Sighle. Come in, master. Come in, Cuimin.

MAOILSHEACHLAINN. No, Maire, we'll sit here a while. You and the children will like to be by yourselves. Go in, west, children. Cuimin and I have plans to make. We're expecting Diarmaid of the Bridge in.

MAIRE. We don't grudge you a share in our joy, master. Nor you, Cuimin.

CUIMIN. No, go on in, Maire. We'll go west after you. We want to talk here.

MAIRE. Well, come in when you have your talk out. There's enough tea on the pot for everybody. In with you, children.

MacDara, Colm, Sighle and Maire go into the room, Sighle carrying the griddle-cakes and Maire the tea.

MAOILSHEACHLAINN. This is great news, MacDara to be back.

CUIMIN. Do you think will he be with us?

MAOILSHEACHLAINN. Is it a boy with that gesture of the head, that proud, laughing

20

gesture, to be a coward or a stag? You don't know the heart of this boy, Cuimin; the love that's in it, and the strength. You don't know the mind he has, so gracious, so full of wisdom. I taught him when he was only a little ladeen. 'Tis a pity that he had ever to go away from us. And yet, I think, his exile has made him a better man. His soul must be full of great remembrances.

CUIMIN. I never knew rightly why he was banished.

MAOILSHEACHLAINN. Songs he was making that were setting the people's hearts on fire.

CUIMIN. Aye, I often heard his songs.

MAOILSHEACHLAINN. They were full of terrible love for the people and of great anger against the Gall. Some said there was irreligion in them and blasphemy against God. But I never saw it, and I don't believe it. There are some would have us believe that God is on the side of the Gall. Well, word came down from Galway or from Dublin that he would be put in prison, and maybe excommunicated if he did not go away. He was only a gossoon of eighteen, or maybe twenty. The priest

21

counselled him to go, and not to bring sorrow on his mother's house. He went away one evening without taking farewell or leave of anyone.

CUIMIN. Where has he been since, I don't know ?

MAOILSHEACHLAINN. In great cities, I'd say, and in lonely places. He has the face of a scholar, or of a priest, or of a clerk, on him. He must have read a lot, and thought a lot, and made a lot of songs.

CUIMIN. I don't know is he as strong a boy as Colm.

MAOILSHEACHLAINN. He's not as robust in himself as Colm is, but there was great strength in the grip of his hand. I'd say that he'd wield a camán or a pike with any boy on the mountain.

CUIMIN. He'll be a great backing to us if he is with us. The people love him on account of the songs he used to make. There's not a man that won't do his bidding.

MAOILSHEACHLAINN. That's so. And his counsel will be useful to us. He'll make better plans than you or I, Cuimin.

CUIMIN. I wonder what's keeping Diarmaid.

THE SINGER

MAOILSHEACHLAINN. Some news that was
at the forge or at the priest's house, maybe.
He went east the road to see if there was
sign of a word from Galway.

CUIMIN. I'll be uneasy till he comes.
(*He gets up and walks to the window and looks
out; Maoilsheachlainn remains deep in thought
by the fire. Cuimin returns from the window
and continues.*) Is it to march we'll do, or
to fight here in the hills?

MAOILSHEACHLAINN. Out Maam Gap
we'll go and meet the boys from the Joyce
country. We'll leave some to guard the Gap
and some at Leenane. We'll march the
road between the lakes, through Maam and
Cornamona and Clonbur to Cong. Then
we'll have friends on our left at Ballinrobe
and on our right at Tuam. What is there
to stop us but the few men the Gall have
in Clifden?

CUIMIN. And if they march against us,
we can destroy them from the mountains.

MAOILSHEACHLAINN. We can. It's into
a trap they'll walk.

*MacDara appears in the doorway of the
room with a cup of tea and some griddle-
cake in his hand.*

23

MacDara. I've brought you out a cup of tea, master. I thought it long you were sitting here.

Maoilsheachlainn (*taking it*). God bless you, MacDara.

MacDara. Go west, Cuimin. There's a place at the table for you now.

Cuimin (*rising and going in*). I may as well. Give me a call, boy, when Diarmaid comes.

Maoilsheachlainn. This is a great day, MacDara.

MacDara. It is a great day and a glad day, and yet it is a sorrowful day.

Maoilsheachlainn. How can the day of your home-coming be sorrowful?

MacDara. Has not every great joy a great sorrow at its core? Does not the joy of home-coming enclose the pain of departing? I have a strange feeling, master, I have only finished a long journey, and I feel as if I were about to take another long journey. I meant this to be a home-coming. but it seems only like a meeting on the way. . . . When my mother stood up to meet me with her arms stretched out to me, I thought of Mary meeting her Son on the Dolorous Way.

MAOILSHEACHLAINN. That was a queer thought. What was it that drew you home?

MACDARA. Some secret thing that I have no name for. Some feeling that I must see my mother, and Colm, and Sighle, again. A feeling that I must face some great adventure with their kisses on my lips. I seemed to see myself brought to die before a great crowd that stood cold and silent; and there were some that cursed me in their hearts for having brought death into their houses. Sad dead faces seemed to reproach me. Oh, the wise, sad faces of the dead— and the keening of women rang in my ears. But I felt that the kisses of those three, warm on my mouth, would be as wine in my blood, strengthening me to bear what men said, and to die with only love and pity in my heart, and no bitterness.

MAOILSHEACHLAINN. It was strange that you should see yourself like that.

MACDARA. It was foolish. One has strange, lonesome thoughts when one is in the middle of crowds. But I am glad of that thought, for it drove me home. I felt so lonely away from here. . . . My mother's hair is greyer than it was.

MAOILSHEACHLAINN. Aye, she has been ageing. She has had great sorrows: your father dead and you banished. Colm is grown a fine, strapping boy.

MACDARA. He is. There is some shyness between Colm and me. We have not spoken yet as we used to.

MAOILSHEACHLAINN. When boys are brought up together and then parted for a long time there is often shyness between them when they meet again. . . . Do you find Sighle changed?

MACDARA. No; and, yet—yes. Master, she is very beautiful. I did not know a woman could be so beautiful. I thought that all beauty was in the heart, that beauty was a secret thing that could be seen only with the eyes of reverie, or in a dream of some unborn splendour. I had schooled myself to think physical beauty an unholy thing. I tried to keep my heart virginal; and sometimes in the street of a city when I have stopped to look at the white limbs of some beautiful child, and have felt the pain that the sight of great beauty brings, I have wished that I could blind my eyes so that I might shut out the sight of everything that tempted me. At times I have rebelled against that, and have cried aloud that God would not have filled the world with beauty, even to the making drunk of the sight, if beauty were not of heaven. But, then, again, I have said, "This is the subtlest form of temptation; this is to give to one's own desire the sanction of God's will." And I have hardened my heart and kept myself cold and chaste as the top of a high mountain. But now I think I was wrong, for beauty like Sighle's must be holy.

MAOILSHEACHLAINN. Surely a good and comely girl is holy. You question yourself too much, MacDara. You brood too much. Do you remember when you were a gossoon, how you cried over the wild duck whose wing you broke by accident with a stone, and made a song about the crane whose nest you found ravished, and about the red robin you found perished on the doorstep? And how the priest laughed because you told him in confession that you had stolen drowned lilies from the river?

MACDARA (*laughing*). Aye, it was at a station in Diarmaid of the Bridge's, and when the priest laughed my face got red, and everyone looked at us, and I got up and ran out of the house.

MAOILSHEACHLAINN (*laughing*). I remember it well. We thought it was what you told him you were in love with his house-keeper.

MACDARA. It's little but I was, too. She used to give me apples out of the priest's apple-garden. Little brown russet apples, the sweetest I ever tasted. I used to think that the apples of the Hesperides that the Children of Tuireann went to quest must have been like them.

MAOILSHEACHLAINN. It's a wonder but you made a poem about them.

MACDARA. I did. I made a poem in Deibhidhe of twenty quatrains.

MAOILSHEACHLAINN. Did you make many songs while you were away?

MACDARA. When I went away first my heart was as if dead and dumb and I could not make any songs. After a little while, when I was going through the sweet, green country, and I used to come to little towns where I'd see children playing, my heart seemed to open again like hard ground that would be watered with rain. The first song

28

that I made was about the children that I
saw playing in the street of Kilconnell.
The next song that I made was about an
old dark man that I met on the causeway
of Aughrim. I made a glad, proud song
when I saw the broad Shannon flow under
the bridge of Athlone. I made many a
song after that before I reached Dublin.

MAOILSHEACHLAINN. How did it fare
with you in Dublin?

MACDARA. I went to a bookseller and
gave him the book of my songs to print.
He said that he dared not print them; that
the Gall would put him in prison and break
up his printing-press. I was hungry and I
wandered through the streets. Then a man
who saw me read an Irish poster on the
wall spoke to me and asked me where I
came from. I told him my story. In a
few days he came to me and said that he
had found work for me to teach Irish and
Latin and Greek in a school. I went to
the school and taught in it for a year. I
wrote a few poems and they were printed in
a paper. One day the Brother who was
over the school came to me and asked me
was it I that had written those poems. I

29

said it was. He told me then that I could not teach in the school any longer. So I went away.

MAOILSHEACHLAINN. What happened to you after that?

MacDara. I wandered in the streets until I saw a notice that a teacher was wanted to teach a boy. I went to the house and a lady engaged me to teach her little son for ten shillings a week. Two years I spent at that. The boy was a winsome child, and he grew into my heart. I thought it a wonderful thing to have the moulding of a mind, of a life, in my hands. Do you ever think that, you who are a schoolmaster?

MAOILSHEACHLAINN. It's not much time I get for thinking.

MacDara. I have done nothing all my life but think : think and make poems.

MAOILSHEACHLAINN. If the thoughts and the poems are good, that is a good life's work.

MacDara. Aye, they say that to be busy with the things of the spirit is better than to be busy with the things of the body. But I am not sure, master. Can the Vision

Beautiful alone content a man ? I think
true man is divine in this, that, like God,
he must needs create, he must needs do.

MAOILSHEACHLAINN. Is not a poet a
maker ?

MACDARA. No, he is only a voice that
cries out, a sigh that trembles into rest.
The true teacher must suffer and do. He
must break bread to the people : he must
go into Gethsemane and toil up the steep of
Golgotha. . . . Sometimes I think that
to be a woman and to serve and suffer as
women do is to be the highest thing.
Perhaps that is why I felt it proud and
wondrous to be a teacher, for a teacher does
that. I gave to the little lad I taught the
very flesh and blood and breath that were
my life. I fed him on the milk of my
kindness ; I breathed into him my spirit.

MAOILSHEACHLAINN. Did he repay you
for that great service ?

MACDARA. Can any child repay its
mother ? Master, your trade is the most
sorrowful of all trades. You are like a poor
mother who spends herself in nursing children who go away and never come back to
her.

31

MAOILSHEACHLAINN. Was your little pupil untrue to you?

MACDARA. Nay; he was so true to me that his mother grew jealous of me. A good mother and a good teacher are always jealous of each other. That is why a teacher's trade is the most sorrowful of all trades. If he is a bad teacher his pupil *wanders* away from him. If he is a good teacher his pupil's folk grow jealous of him. My little pupil's mother bade him choose between her and me.

MAOILSHEACHLAINN. Which did he choose?

MACDARA. He chose his mother. How could I blame him?

MAOILSHEACHLAINN. What did you do?

MACDARA. I shouldered my bundle and took to the roads.

MAOILSHEACHLAINN. How did it fare with you?

MACDARA. It fares ill with one who is so poor that he has no longer even his dreams. I was the poorest *shuiler* on the roads of Ireland, for I had no single illusion left to me. I could neither pray when I came to a holy well nor drink in a public-house when I had got a little money. One seemed to me as foolish as the other.

MAOILSHEACHLAINN. Did you make no songs in those days?

MACDARA. I made one so bitter that when I recited it at a wake they thought I was some wandering, wicked spirit, and they put me out of the house.

MAOILSHEACHLAINN. Did you not pray at all?

MACDARA. Once, as I knelt by the cross of Kilgobbin, it became clear to me, with an awful clearness, that there was no God. Why pray after that? I burst into a fit of laughter at the folly of men in thinking that there is a God. I felt inclined to run through the villages and cry aloud, "People, it is all a mistake; there is no God."

MAOILSHEACHLAINN. MacDara, this grieves me.

MACDARA. Then I said, "why take away their illusion? If they find out that there is no God, their hearts will be as lonely as mine." So I walked the roads with my secret.

MAOILSHEACHLAINN. MacDara, I am sorry for this. You must pray, you must pray.

33   D

You will find God again. He has only hidden His face from you.

MacDara. No, He has revealed His Face to me. His Face is terrible and sweet, Maoilsheachlainn. I know It well now.

Maoilsheachlainn. Then you found Him again?

MacDara. His Name is suffering. His Name is loneliness. His Name is abjection.

Maoilsheachlainn. I do not rightly understand you, and yet I think you are saying something that is true.

MacDara. I have lived with the homeless and with the breadless. Oh, Maoilsheachlainn, the poor, the poor! I have seen such sad childings, such bare marriage feasts, such candleless wakes! In the pleasant country places I have seen them, but oftener in the dark, unquiet streets of the city. My heart has been heavy with the sorrow of mothers, my eyes have been wet with the tears of children. The people, Maoilsheachlainn, the dumb, suffering people: reviled and outcast, yet pure and splendid and faithful. In them I saw, or seemed to see again, the Face of God. Ah, it is a tear-stained face,

34

blood-stained, defiled with ordure, but it is the Holy Face!

.   .   .   .

There is a page of MS. missing here, which evidently covered the exit to the room of MacDara and the entrance of Diarmaid.

MAOILSHEACHLAINN. What news have you with you?

DIARMAID. The Gall have marched from Clifden.

MAOILSHEACHLAINN. Is it into the hills?

DIARMAID. By Letterfrack they have come, and the Pass of Kylemore, and through Glen Inagh.

COLM. And no word from Galway yet?

DIARMAID. No word, nor sign of a word.

COLM. They told us to wait for the word. We've waited too long.

MAOILSHEACHLAINN. The messenger may have been caught. Perhaps the Gall are marching from Galway too.

COLM. We'd best strike ourselves, so.

CUIMIN. Is it to strike before the word is given?

COLM. Is it to die like rats you'd have us because the word is not given?

CUIMIN. Our plans are not finished ; our orders are not here.

COLM. Our plans will never be finished. Our orders may never be here.

CUIMIN. We've no one to lead us.

COLM. Didn't you elect me your captain?

CUIMIN. We did : but not to bid us rise out when the whole country is quiet. We were to get the word from the men that are over the people. They'll speak when the time comes.

COLM. They should have spoken before the Gall marched.

CUIMIN. What call have you to say what they should or what they should not have done? Am I speaking lie or truth, men? Are we to rise out before the word comes? I say we must wait for the word. What do you say, Diarmaid, you that was our messenger to Galway?

DIARMAID. I like the way Colm has spoken, and we may live to say that he spoke wisely as well as bravely ; but I'm slow to give my voice to send out the boys of this mountain—our poor little handful—

36

to stand with their poor pikes against the big guns of the Gall. If we had news that they were rising in the other countrysides ; but we've got no news.

CUIMIN. What do you say, master? You're wiser than any of us.

MAOILSHEACHLAINN. I say to Colm that a greater one than he or I may give us the word before the day is old. Let you have patience, Colm —

COLM. My mother told me to have patience this morning, when MacDara's step was on the street. Patience, and I after waiting seven years before I spoke, and then to speak too late !

MAOILSHEACHLAINN. What are you saying at all?

COLM. I am saying this, master, that I'm going out the road to meet the Gall, if only five men of the mountain follow me.

Sighle has appeared in the doorway and stands terror-stricken.

CUIMIN. You will not, Colm.

COLM. I will.

DIARMAID. This is throwing away men's lives.

COLM. Men's lives get very precious to

37

them when they have bought out their land.

MAOILSHEACHLAINN. Listen to me, Colm —

Colm goes out angrily, and the others follow him, trying to restrain him. Sighle comes to the fire, where she kneels.

SIGHLE (*as in a reverie*). "They will go out laughing," I said, but Colm has gone out with anger in his heart. And he was so kind. . . . Love is a terrible thing. There is no pain so great as the pain of love. . . . I wish MacDara and I were children in the green *mám* and that we did not know that we loved each other. . . Colm will lie dead on the road to Glen Inagh, and MacDara will go out to die. . . . There is nothing in the world but love and death.

MacDara comes out of the room.

MACDARA (*in a low voice*). She has dropped asleep, Sighle.

SIGHLE. She watched long, MacDara. We all watched long.

MACDARA. Every long watch ends. Every traveller comes home.

SIGHLE. Sometimes when people watch it is death that comes.

38

MacDara. Could there be a royaller coming, Sighle? . . . Once I wanted life. You and I to be together in one place always : that is what I wanted. But now I see that we shall be together for a little time only ; that I have to do a hard, sweet thing, and that I must do it alone. And because I love you I would not have it different. . . . I wanted to have your kiss on my lips, Sighle, as well as my mother's and Colm's. But I will deny myself that. (*Sighle is crying.*) Don't cry, child. Stay near my mother while she lives—it may be for a little while of years. You poor women suffer so much pain, so much sorrow, and yet you do not die until long after your strong, young sons and lovers have died.

Maire's voice is heard from the room, crying : MacDara !

MacDara. She is calling me.

He goes into the room ; Sighle cries on her knees by the fire. After a little while voices are heard outside, the latch is lifted, and Maoilsheachlainn comes in.

Sighle. Is he gone, master ?

Maoilsheachlainn. Gone out the road

with ten or fifteen of the young lads. Is
MacDara within still?

SIGHLE.' He was here in the kitchen
a while. His mother called him and he
went back to her.

*Maoilsheachlainn goes over and sits down
near the fire.*

MAOILSHEACHLAINN. I think, maybe, that
Colm did what was right. We are too old
to be at the head of work like this. Was
MacDara talking to you about the trouble?

SIGHLE. He said that he would have to do
a hard, sweet thing, and that he would have
to do it alone.

MAOILSHEACHLAINN. I'm sorry but I
called him before Colm went out.

*A murmur is heard as of a crowd of men
talking as they come up the hill.*

SIGHLE. What is that noise like voices?

MAOILSHEACHLAINN. It is the boys coming
up the hillside. There was a great crowd
gathering below at the cross.

*The voices swell loud outside the door. Cuimin
Eanna, Diarmaid, and some others come in.*

DIARMAID. The men say we did wrong
to let Colm go out with that little handful.
They say we should all have marched.

40

Cuimin. And I say Colm was wrong to go before he got his orders. Are we all to go out and get shot down because one man is hotheaded? Where is the plan that was to come from Galway?

Maoilsheachlainn. Men, I'm blaming myself for not saying the thing I'm going to say before we let Colm go. We talk about getting word from Galway. What would you say, neighbours, if the man that will give the word is under the roof of this house.

Cuimin. Who is it you mean?

Maoilsheachlainn (*going to the door of the room and throwing it open*). Let you rise out, MacDara, and reveal yourself to the men that are waiting for your word.

One of the Newcomers. Has MacDara come home?

MacDara comes out of the room: Maire ni Fhiannachta stands behind him in the doorway.

Diarmaid (*starting up from where he has been sitting*). That is the man that stood among the people in the fair of Uachtar Ard! (*He goes up to MacDara and kisses his hand.*)

I could not get near you yesterday, MacDara, with the crowds that were round you. What was on me that didn't know you? Sure, I had a right to know that sad, proud head. Maire ni Fhiannachta, men and women yet unborn will bless the pains of your first childing.

Maire ni Fhiannachta comes forward slowly and takes her son's hand and kisses it.

MAIRE (*in a low voice*). Soft hand that played at my breast, strong hand that will fall heavy on the Gall, brave hand that will break the yoke! Men of this mountain, my son MacDara is the Singer that has quickened the dead years and all the quiet dust! Let the horsemen that sleep in Aileach rise up and follow him into the war! Weave your winding-sheets, women, for there will be many a noble corpse to be waked before the new moon!

Each comes forward and kisses his hand.

MAOILSHEACHLAINN. Let you speak, MacDara, and tell us is it time.

MACDARA. Where is Colm?

DIARMAID. Gone out the road to fight the Gall, himself and fifteen.

42

MacDara. Has not Colm spoken by his deed already?

Cuimin. You are our leader.

MacDara. Your leader is the man that spoke first. Give me a pike and I will follow Colm. Why did you let him go out with fifteen men only? You are fourscore on the mountain.

Diarmaid. We thought it a foolish thing for fourscore to go into battle against four thousand, or, maybe, forty thousand.

MacDara. And so it is a foolish thing. Do you want us to be wise?

Cuimin. This is strange talk.

MacDara. I will talk to you more strangely yet. It is for your own souls' sakes I would have had the fourscore go, and not for Colm's sake, or for the battle's sake, for the battle is won whether you go or not.

*A cry is heard outside. One rushes in
terror-stricken.*

The Newcomer. Young Colm has fallen at the Glen foot.

MacDara. The fifteen were too many. Old men, you did not do your work well enough. You should have kept all back but

THE KING

A green before the monastery. The voices of monks are heard chanting. Through the chanting breaks the sound of a trumpet. A little boy runs out from the monastery and stands on the green looking in the direction whence the trumpet has spoken.

THE BOY. Conall, Diarmaid, Giolla na Naomh!

The voices of other boys answer him.

FIRST BOY. There is a host marching from the North.

SECOND BOY. Where is it?

FIRST BOY. See it beneath you in the glen.

THIRD BOY. It is the King's host.

FOURTH BOY. The King is going to battle.

The trumpet speaks again, nearer. The boys go upon the rampart of the monastery. The murmur of a marching host is heard.

FIRST BOY. I see the horses and the riders.

FOURTH BOY. He has a keen-edged, gold-hilted sword and a mighty-shafted, blue-headed spear and a glorious red-emblazoned shield. I saw him once in my father's house.

FIRST BOY. What was he like?

FOURTH BOY. He was tall and noble. He was strong and broad-shouldered. He had long fair hair. He had a comely proud face. He had two piercing grey eyes. A white vest of satin next his skin. A very beautiful red tunic, with a white hood, upon his body. A royal mantle of purple about him. Seven colours upon him, between vest and tunic and hood and mantle. A silver brooch upon his breast. A kingly diadem upon his head, and the colour of gold upon it. Two great wings rising above his head, as white as the two wings of a sea-gull and as broad as the two wings of an eagle. He was a gallant man.

SECOND BOY. And what was the look of his face?

THIRD BOY. Did he look angry, stern?

FOURTH BOY. He did, at times.

FIRST BOY. Had he a laughing look?

FOURTH BOY. He laughed only once.

SECOND BOY. How did he look mostly? Stern or laughing?

FOURTH BOY. He looked sorrowful. When he was talking to the kings and the heroes he had an angry and a laughing look every second while, but when he was silent he was sorrowful.

FIRST BOY. What sorrow can he have?

FOURTH BOY. I do not know. The thousands he has slain, perhaps.

SECOND BOY. The churches he has plundered.

THIRD BOY. The battles he has lost.

GIOLLA NA NAOMH. Alas, the poor King!

SECOND BOY. You would not like to be a King, Giolla na Naomh?

GIOLLA NA NAOMH. I would not. I would rather be a monk that I might pray for the King.

FOURTH BOY. I may have the kingship of this country when I am a man, for my father is of the royal blood.

SECOND BOY. And my father is of the royal blood, too.

THIRD BOY. Aye, and mine.

FOURTH BOY. I will not let the kingdom go with either of you. It is mine!

50

SECOND BOY. It is not, but mine

THIRD BOY. It matters not whose it is, for *I* will have it!

SECOND BOY. No, nor anyone of your house!

FOURTH BOY (*seizing a switch of sally and brandishing it*). I will ply the venom of my sword upon you! I will defend my kingdom against my enemies! Giolla na Naomh, pray for the King!

A bell sounds from the monastery.

GIOLLA NA NAOMH. The bell is ringing.

The people of the monastery come upon the green in ones and twos, the Abbot last. The boys gather a little apart. Distant sounds of battle are heard.

THE ABBOT. My children, the King is giving battle to his foes.

FIRST MONK. This King has lost every battle into which he has gone up to this.

THE ABBOT. In a vision that I saw last night as I knelt before my God it was revealed to me that the battle will be broken on the King again.

SECOND MONK. My grief!

THIRD MONK. My grief!

FIRST MONK. Tell us, Father, the cause of these unnumbered defeats.

THE ABBOT. Do you think that an offering will be accepted from polluted hands? This King has shed the blood of the innocent. He has made spoils and forays. He has oppressed the poor. He has forsaken the friendship of God and made friends with evil-doers.

FIRST MONK. That is true. Yet it is a good fight that the King fights now, for he gives battle for his people.

THE ABBOT. It is an angel that should be sent to pour out the wine and to break the bread of this sacrifice. Not by an unholy King should the noble wine that is in the veins of good heroes be spilt; not at the behest of a guilty king should fair bodies be mangled. I say to you that the offering will not be accepted.

FIRST MONK. And are all guilty of the sins of the King? If the King is defeated it's grief will be for all. Why must all suffer for the sins of the King? On the King the eric!

THE ABBOT. The nation is guilty of the sins of its princes. I say to you that this nation shall not be freed until it chooses for itself a righteous King.

SECOND MONK. Where shall a righteous King be found?

THE ABBOT. I do not know, unless he be found among these little boys.

The boys have drawn near and are gathered about the Abbot.

FIRST MONK. And shall the people be in bondage until these little lads are fit for battle? It is not the King's case I pity, but the case of the people. I heard women mourning last night. Shall women be mourning in this land till doom?

THIRD MONK. As I went out from the monastery yesterday there was a dead man on the verge of the wood. Battle is terrible.

SECOND MONK. No, battle is glorious! While we were singing our None but now, Father, I heard, through the psalmody of the brethren, the voice of a trumpet. My heart leaped, and I would fain have risen from the place where I was and gone after that gallant music. I should not have cared though it were to my death I went.

THE ABBOT. That is the voice of a young man. The old wait for death, but the

young go to meet it. If into this quiet
place, where monks chant and children play,
there were to come from yonder battlefield a bloodstained man, calling upon all
to follow him into the battle-press, there is
none here that would not rise and follow
him, but I myself and the old brother that
rings our bell. There is none of you,
young brothers, no, nor any of these little
lads, that would not rise from me and go
into the battle. That music of the fighters
makes drunk the hearts of young men.

SECOND MONK. It is good for young men
to be made drunk.

FIRST MONK. Brother, you speak wicked-
ness.

THE ABBOT. There is a heady ale which
all young men should drink, for he who
has not been made drunk with it has not
lived. It is with that ale that God makes
drunk the hearts of the saints. I would not
forbid you your intoxication, O young men!

FIRST MONK. This is not plain, Father.

THE ABBOT. Do you think if that terrible,
beautiful voice for which young men strain
their ears were to speak from yon place
where the fighters are, and the horses, and

the music, that I would stay you, did ye rise to obey it? Do you think I would grudge any of you? Do you think I would grudge the dearest of these little boys, to death calling with that terrible, beautiful voice? I would let you all go, though I and the old brother should be very lonely here.

SECOND BOY. Giolla na Naomh would not go, Father.

THE ABBOT. Why do you say that?

SECOND BOY. He said that he would rather be a monk.

THE ABBOT. Would you not go into the battle, Giolla na Naomh?

GIOLLA NA NAOMH. I would. I would go as a gilly to the King, that I might serve him when all would forsake him.

THE ABBOT. But it is to the saints you are gilly, Giolla na Naomh, and not to the King.

GIOLLA NA NAOMH. It were not much for the poor King to have one little gilly that would not forsake him when the battle would be broken on him and all forsaking him.

THE ABBOT. This child is right. While we think of glory he thinks of service.

An outcry as of grief and dismay is heard from the battlefield.

FIRST MONK. I fear me that the King is beaten !

THE ABBOT. Go upon the rampart and tell us what you see.

FIRST MONK (*having gone upon the rampart*). A man comes towards us in flight.

SECOND MONK. What manner of man is he ?

FIRST MONK. A bloodstained man, all spent, his feet staggering and stumbling under him.

SECOND MONK. Is he a man of the King's people ?

FIRST MONK. He is.

A soldier comes upon the green all spent.

THE SOLDIER. The King is beaten !

THE MONKS. My sorrow, my sorrow !

THE SOLDIER. The King is beaten, I say to you ! O ye of the books and the bells, small was your help to us in the hard battle ! The King is beaten !

THE ABBOT. Where is the King ?

THE SOLDIER. He is flying.

THE ABBOT. Give us the description of the battle.

THE SOLDIER. I cannot speak. Let a drink be given to me.

THE ABBOT. Let a drink be given to this man.

The little boy who is called Giolla na Naomh gives him a drink of water.

THE ABBOT. Speak to us now and give us the description of the battle.

THE SOLDIER. Each man of us was a fighter of ten. The King was a fighter of a hundred. But what availed us our valour? We were beaten and we fled. Hundreds lie sole to sole on the lea.

THE MONKS. My sorrow ! My sorrow !

A din grows.

SECOND MONK. Who comes ?

FIRST MONK. The King !

Riders and gillies come upon the green pell-mell, the King in their midst. The King goes upon his knees before the Abbot, and throws his sword upon the ground.

THE KING. Give me your curse, O man of God, and let me go to my death ! I am beaten. My people are beaten. Ten battles have I fought against my foes, and every battle of them has been broken on me. It is I who have brought God's wrath upon this land. Ask your God not to wreak his

57

anger on my people henceforth, but to wreak it on me. Have pity on my people, O man of God !

THE ABBOT. God will have pity on them.

THE KING. God has forsaken me.

THE ABBOT. You have forsaken God.

THE KING. God has forsaken my people.

THE ABBOT. He has not, neither will He. He will save this nation if it choose a righteous King.

THE KING. Give it then a righteous King. Give it one of your monks or one of these little lads to be its King. The battle on your protection, O man of God !

THE ABBOT. Not so, but on the protection of the sword of a righteous King. Speak to me, my children, and tell me who among you is the most righteous ?

FIRST MONK. I have sinned.

SECOND MONK. And I.

THIRD MONK. Father, we have all sinned.

THE ABBOT. I, too, have sinned. All that are men have sinned. How soon we exchange the wisdom of children for the folly of men ! O wise children, busy with your toys while we are busy with our sins ! I see clearly now. I shall find a sinless

King among these little boys. Speak to
me, boys, and tell me who is most innocent
among you?

THE BOYS (*with one voice*). Giolla na
Naomh.

THE ABBOT. The little lad that waits
upon all! Ye are right. The last shall be
first. Giolla na Naomh, will you be King
over this nation?

GIOLLA NA NAOMH. I am too young,
Father, I am too weak.

THE ABBOT. Come hither to me, child.
(*The child goes over to him.*) O fosterling that
I have nourished, if I ask this thing of you,
will you not do it?

GIOLLA NA NAOMH. I will be obedient
to you, Father.

THE ABBOT. Will you turn your face
into the battle?

GIOLLA NA NAOMH. I will do the duty
of a King.

THE ABBOT. Little one, it may be that
your death will come of it.

GIOLLA NA NAOMH. Welcome is death
if it be appointed to me.

THE ABBOT. Did I not say that the
young seek death? They are spendthrift

59

of all that we hoard jealously; they pursue all that we shun. The terrible, beautiful voice has spoken to this child. O herald death, you shall be answered! I will not grudge you my fosterling.

THE KING. Abbot, I will fight my own battles: no child shall die for me!

THE ABBOT. You have given me your sword, and I give it to this child. God has spoken through the voice of His ancient herald, the terrible, beautiful voice that comes out of the heart of battles.

GIOLLA NA NAOMH. Let me do this little thing, King. I will guard your banner well. I will bring you back your sword after the battle. I am only your little gilly, who watches while the tired King sleeps. I will sleep to-night while you shall watch.

THE KING. My pity, my three pities!

GIOLLA NA NAOMH. We slept last night while you were marching through the dark country. Poor King, your marchings have been long. My march will be very short.

THE ABBOT. Let this gentle asking prevail with you, King. I say to you that God has spoken.

THE KING. I do not understand your God.

THE KING

THE ABBOT. Who understands Him? He
demands not understanding, but obedience.
This child is obedient, and because he is
obedient, God will do mighty things through
him. King, you must yield to this.

THE KING. I yield, I yield! Woe is
me that I did not fall in yonder onset!

THE ABBOT. Let this child be stripped
that the raiment of a King may be put
about him. (*The child is stripped of his
clothing.*) Let a royal vest be put next the
skin of the child. (*A royal vest is put upon
him.*) Let a royal tunic be put about him.
(*A royal tunic is put about him above the vest,
and sandals upon his feet.*) Let the royal
mantle be put about him. (*The King takes
off the royal mantle and it is put upon the child.*)
Let a royal diadem be put upon his head.
(*The King takes off the royal diadem and it is
put upon the child's head.*) Let him be given
the shield of the King. (*The shieldbearer
holds up the shield.*) A blessing on this
shield! May it be firm against foes!

THE HEROES. A blessing on this shield!
The shield is put on the child's left arm.

THE ABBOT. Let him be given the spear
of the King. (*The spearbearer comes forward

61

and holds up the spear.) A blessing on this spear! May it be sharp against foes!

THE HEROES. A blessing on this spear!

THE ABBOT. Let him be given the sword of the King. (*The King lifts his sword and girds it round the child's waist. Giolla na Naomh draws the sword and holds it in his right hand.*) A blessing on this sword! May it be hard to smite foes!

THE HEROES. A blessing on this sword!

THE ABBOT. I call this little lad King, and I put the battle under his protection in the name of God.

THE KING (*kneeling before the boy*). I do homage to thee, O King, and I put the battle under thy protection.

THE HEROES, MONKS, BOYS, etc. (*kneeling*). We do homage to thee, O King, and we put the battle under thy protection.

GIOLLA NA NAOMH. I undertake to sustain the battle in the name of God.

THE ABBOT. Let a steed be brought him. (*A steed is brought.*) Let the banner of the King be unfurled. (*The banner is unfurled.*) Turn thy face to the battle, O King!

GIOLLA NA NAOMH (*kneeling*). Bless me, Father.

THE ABBOT. A blessing on thee, little one.

THE HEROES, etc. (*with one voice*). Take victory in battle and slaying, O King.

The little King mounts, and, with the heroes and soldiers and gillies, rides to the battle. The Abbot, the King, the Monks, and the Boys watch them.

THE ABBOT. King, I have given you the noblest jewel that was in my house. I loved yonder child.

THE KING. Priest, I have never received from my tributary kings a kinglier gift.

FIRST MONK. They have reached the place of battle.

THE ABBOT. O strong God, make strong the hand of this child. Make firm his foot. Make keen his sword. Let the purity of his heart and the humbleness of his spirit be unto him a magnifying of courage and an exaltation of mind. Ye angels that fought the ancient battles, ye veterans of God, make a battle-pen about him and fight before him with flaming swords.

THE MONKS AND BOYS. Amen, Amen.

THE ABBOT. O God, save this nation by the sword of the sinless boy.

THE KING. And O Christ, that was

crucified on the hill, bring the child safe from the perilous battle.

THE ABBOT. King, King, freedom is not purchased but with a great price. (*A trumpet speaks.*) Let the description of the battle be given us.

The First Monk and the Second Monk go upon the rampart.

FIRST MONK. The two hosts are face to face. *Another trumpet speaks.*

SECOND MONK. That is sweet ! It is the trumpet of the King ! *Shouts.*

FIRST MONK. The King's host raises shouts. *Other shouts.*

SECOND MONK. The enemy answers them.

FIRST MONK. The hosts advance against each other.

SECOND MONK. They fight.

FIRST MONK. Our people are yielding.

THIRD MONK. Say not so.

SECOND MONK. My grief, they are yielding. *A trumpet speaks.*

THIRD MONK. Sweet again ! It is timely spoken, O trumpet of the King !

FIRST MONK. The King's banner is going into the battle !

SECOND MONK. I see the little King !

64

THIRD MONK. Is he going into the battle?

FIRST MONK. Yes.

THE MONKS AND BOYS (*with one voice*). Take victory in battle and slaying, O King!

SECOND MONK. It is a good fight now.

FIRST MONK. Two seas have met on the plain.

SECOND MONK. Two raging seas!

FIRST MONK. One sea rolls back.

SECOND MONK. It is the enemy that retreats!

FIRST MONK. The little King goes through them.

SECOND MONK. He goes through them like a hawk through small birds.

FIRST MONK. Yea, like a wolf through a flock of sheep on a plain.

SECOND MONK. Like a torrent through a mountain gap.

FIRST MONK. It is a road of rout before him.

SECOND MONK. There are great uproars in the battle. It is a roaring path down which the King rides.

FIRST MONK. O golden head above the slaughter! O shining, terrible sword of the King!

SECOND MONK. The enemy flies!

FIRST MONK. They are beaten! They are beaten! It is a red road of rout! Raise shouts of exultation!

SECOND MONK. My grief!

FIRST MONK. My grief! My grief!

THE ABBOT. What is that?

FIRST MONK. The little King is down!

THE ABBOT. Has he the victory?

FIRST MONK. Yes, but he himself is down. I do not see his golden head. I do not see his shining sword. My grief! They raise his body from the plain.

THE ABBOT. Is the enemy flying?

SECOND MONK. Yes, they fly. They are pursued. They are scattered. They are scattered as a mist would be scattered. They are no longer seen on the plain.

THE ABBOT. It's thanks to God! (*Keening is heard.*) Thou hast been answered, O terrible voice! Old herald, my foster child has answered!

THIRD MONK. They bear hither a dead child.

THE KING. He said that he would sleep to-night and that I should watch.

Heroes come upon the green bearing the body of Giolla na Naomh on a bier ; there

66

are women keening it. The bier is laid in the centre of the green.

THE KING. He has brought me back my sword. He has guarded my banner well.

THE ABBOT (*lifting the sword from the bier*). Take the sword.

THE KING. No, I will let him keep it. A King should sleep with a sword. This was a very valiant King. (*He takes the sword from the Abbot and lays it again upon the bier. He kneels.*) I do homage to thee, O dead King, O victorious child! I kiss thee, O white body, since it is thy purity that hath redeemed my people. (*He kisses the forehead of Giolla na Naomh. They commence to keen again.*)

THE ABBOT. Do not keen this child, for he hath purchased freedom for his people. Let shouts of exultation be raised and let a canticle be sung in praise of God.

The body is borne into the monastery with a Te Deum.

THE SCENE CLOSES.

THE MASTER

*A little cloister in a woodland. The
subdued sunlight of a forest place comes
through the arches. On the left, one arch
gives a longer vista where the forest opens
and the sun shines upon a far hill. In
the centre of the cloister two or three steps
lead to an inner place, as it were a little
chapel or cell.*

*Art, Breasal, and Maine are busy with
a game of jackstones about the steps. They
play silently.*

Ronan enters from the left.

RONAN. Where is the Master?

ART. He has not left his cell yet.

RONAN. He is late. Who is with him, Art?

ART. I was with him till a while ago.
When he had finished his thanksgiving he
told me he had one other little prayer to
say which he could not leave over. He
said it was for a soul that was in danger. I
left him on his knees and came out into the
sunshine.

MAINE. Aye, you knew that Breasal and I were here with the jackstones.

BREASAL. I served his Mass yesterday, and he stayed praying so long after it that I fell asleep. I did not stir till he laid his hand upon my shoulder. Then I started up and said I, " Is that you, little mother?" He laughed and said he, "No, Breasal, it's no one so good as your mother."

RONAN. He is merry and gentle this while back, although he prays and fasts longer than he used to. Little Iollann says he tells him the merriest stories.

BREASAL.. He is fond of little Iollann.

MAINE. Aye; when Iollann is late, or when he is inattentive, the Master pretends not to notice it.

BREASAL. Well, Iollann is only a little lad.

MAINE. He is more like a little maid, with his fair cheek that reddens when the Master speaks to him.

ART. Faith, you wouldn't call him a little maid when you'd see him strip to swim a river.

RONAN. Or when you'd see him spring up to meet the ball in a hurley match.

72

MAINE. He has, certainly, many accomplishments.

BREASAL. He has a high, manly heart.

MAINE. He has a beautiful white body, and, therefore, you all love him; aye, the Master and all. We have no woman here and so we make love to our little Iollann.

RONAN (*laughing*). Why, I thrashed him ere-yesterday for putting magories down my neck!

MAINE. Men sometimes thrash their women, Ronan. It is one of the ways of loving.

ART. Maine, you have been listening to some satirist making satires. There was once a Maine that was called Maine Honeymouth. You will be called Maine Bitter-Tongue.

MAINE. Well, I've won this game of jackstones. Will you play another?

CEALLACH (*enters hastily*). Lads, do you know what I have seen?

ART. What is it, Ceallach?

CEALLACH. A host of horsemen riding through the dark of the wood. A grim host, with spears.

MAINE. The King goes hunting.

73

CEALLACH. My grief for the noble deer that the King hunts!

BREASAL. What deer is that?

CEALLACH. Our Master, Ciaran.

RONAN. I heard one of the captains say that the cell was to be surrounded.

ART. But why does the King come against Ciaran?

CEALLACH. It is the Druids that have incited him. They say that Ciaran is over-turning the ancient law of the people.

MAINE. The King has ordered him to leave the country.

BREASAL. Aye, there was a King's Messenger here the other day who spoke long to the Master.

ART. It is since then that the Master has been praying so long every day.

RONAN. Is he afraid that the King will kill him?

ART. No, it is for a soul that is in danger that he prays. Is it the King's soul that is in danger?

MAINE. Hush, the Master is coming.

CIARAN (*comes out from the inner place; the pupils rise*). Are all here?

BREASAL. Iollann Beag has not come yet.

CIARAN. Not yet?

CEALLACH. Master, the King's horsemen are in the wood.

CIARAN. I hope no evil has chanced to little Iollann.

MAINE. What evil could chance to him?

CEALLACH. Master, the King is seeking you in the wood.

CIARAN. Does he not know where my cell is?

BREASAL. The King has been stirred up against you, Master, rise and fly before the horsemen surround the cell.

CIARAN. No, if the King seeks me he will find me here. . . . I wish little Iollann were come. (*The voice of Iollann Beag is heard singing. All listen.*) That is his voice.

ART. He always comes singing.

MAINE. Aye, he sings profane songs in the very church porch.

RONAN. Which is as bad as if one were to play with jackstones on the church steps.

CIARAN. I am glad little Iollann has come safe.

Iollann Beag comes into the cloister singing.

IOLLANN BEAG (*sings*).

We watch the wee ladybird fly far away,
With an óró and an iero and an úmbó éró.

ART. Hush, Iollann. You are in God's
place.

IOLLANN BEAG. Does God not like music?
Why then did he make the finches and the
chafers?

MAINE. Your song is profane.

IOLLANN BEAG. I didn't know.

CIARAN. Nay, Maine, no song is profane
unless there be profanity in the heart. But
why do you come so late, Iollann Beag?

IOLLANN BEAG. There was a high oak
tree that I had never climbed. I went up
to its top, and swung myself to the top of
the next tree. I saw the tops of all the
trees like the green waves of the sea.

CIARAN. Little truant!

IOLLANN BEAG. I am sorry, Master.

CIARAN. Nay, I am not vext with you.
But you must not climb tall trees again at
lesson time. We have been waiting for
you. Let us begin our lesson, lads.

He sits down.

CEALLACH. Dear Master, I ask you to fly

from this place ere the King's horsemen close you in.

CIARAN. My boy, you must not tempt me. He is a sorry champion who forsakes his place of battle. This is my place of battle. You would not have me do a coward thing?

ART. But the King has many horsemen. It is not cowardly for one to fly before a host.

CIARAN. Has not the high God captains and legions? What are the King's horsemen to the heavenly riders?

CEALLACH. O my dear Master! —

RONAN. Let be, Ceallach. You cannot move him.

CIARAN. Of what were we to speak to-day? *They have sat down around him.*

ART. You said you would speak of the friends of Our Lord.

CIARAN. Aye, I would speak of friendship and kindly fellowship. Is it not a sad thing that every good fellowship is broken up? No league that is made among men has more than its while, its little, little while. Even that little league of twelve in Galilee was broken full soon. The shepherd was struck and the sheep of the flock scattered. The

77

hardest thing Our dear Lord had to bear was the scattering of His friends.

IOLLANN BEAG. Were none faithful to Him?

CIARAN. One man only and a few women.

IOLLANN BEAG. Who was the man?

CEALLACH. I know! It was John, the disciple that He loved.

CIARAN. Aye, John of the Bosom they call him, for he was Iosa's bosom friend. Can you tell me the names of any others of His friends?

ART. There was James, his brother.

RONAN. There was Lazarus, for whom He wept.

BREASAL. There was Mary, the poor woman that loved Him.

MAINE. There was her sister Martha, who busied herself to make Him comfortable; and the other Mary.

CEALLACH. Mary and Martha; but that other Mary is only a name.

CIARAN. Nay, she was the mother of the sons of Zebedee. She stands for all lowly, hidden women, all the nameless women of the world who are just the mothers of their children. And so we name her one of the

78

three great Marys, with poor Mary that sinned, and with Mary of the Sorrows, the greatest of the Marys. What other friends can you tell me of?

IOLLANN BEAG. There was John the Baptist, His little playmate.

CIARAN. That is well said. Those two Johns were good comrades to Iosa.

RONAN. There was Thomas.

CIARAN. Poor, doubting Thomas. I am glad you did not leave him out.

MAINE. There was Judas who betrayed Him.

ART. There was Peter who —

IOLLANN BEAG. Aye, good Peter of the Sword!

CIARAN. Nay, Iollann, it is Paul that carries a sword.

IOLLANN BEAG. Peter should have a sword, too. I will not have him cheated of his sword! It was a good blow he struck!

BREASAL. Yet the Lord rebuked him for it.

IOLLANN BEAG. The Lord did wrong to rebuke him. He was always down on Peter.

CIARAN. Peter was fiery, and the Lord was very gentle.

IOLLANN BEAG. But when He wanted a rock to build His church on He had to go to Peter. No John of the Bosom then, but the old swordsman. Paul must yield his sword to Peter. I do not like that Paul.

CIARAN. Paul said many hard things and many dark things. When you understand him, Iollann, you will like him.

MAINE. Let him not arrogate a sword merely because his head was cut off, and Iollann will tolerate him.

CIARAN. Who has brought me a poem to-day? You were to bring me poems of Christ's friends.

BREASAL. I have made a Song for Mary Magdalene. Shall I say it to you?

CIARAN. Do, Breasal.

BREASAL (*chants*).

> O woman of the gleaming hair
> (Wild hair that won men's gaze to thee),
> Weary thou turnest from the common stare,
> For the *shuiler* Christ is calling thee.

> O woman, of the snowy side,
> Many a lover hath lain with thee,
> Yet left thee sad at the morning tide;
> But thy lover Christ shall comfort thee.

80

THE MASTER

O woman with the wild thing's heart,
    Old sin hath set a snare for thee;
In the forest ways forspent thou art,
    But the hunter Christ shall pity thee.

O woman spendthrift of thyself,
    Spendthrift of all the love in thee,
Sold unto sin for little pelf,
    The captain Christ shall ransom thee.

O woman that no lover's kiss
    (Tho' many a kiss was given thee)
Could slake thy love, is it not for this
    The hero Christ shall die for thee?

CIARAN That is a good song, Breasal.
What you have said is true, that love is a
very great thing. I do not think faith will
be denied to him that loves. . . .
Iollann was to make me a song to-day, too.

IOLLANN BEAG. I have made only a little
rann. I couldn't think of rhymes for a
big song.

CIARNN. What do you call your rann?

IOLLANN BEAG. It is the Rann of the
Little Playmate. It is a rann that John the
Baptist made when he was on the way to
Iosa's house one day.

CIARAN. Sing it to us, Iollann.

THE MESSENGER. I bring you greeting from the King.

CIARAN. Take back to him my greeting.

THE MESSENGER. The King has come to make the hunting of this wood.

CIARAN. It is the King's privilege to hunt the woods of the cantred.

THE MESSENGER. Not far from here is a green glade of the forest in which the King with his nobles and good men, his gillies and his runners, has sat down to meat.

CIARAN. May it be a merry sitting for them.

THE MESSENGER. It has seemed to the King an unroyal thing to taste of the cheer of this greenwood while he is at enmity with you; for he has remembered the old saying that friendship is more welcome at meat than ale or music. Therefore, he has sent me to say to you that he has put all enmity out of his heart, and that in token thereof he invites you to share his forest feast, such as it is, you and your pupils.

CIARAN. The King is kind. I would like well to come to him, but my rule forbids me to leave this house.

THE MESSENGER. The King will take

badly any refusal. It is not usual to refuse a King's invitation.

CIARAN. When I came to this place, after journeying many long roads of land and sea, I said to myself: "I will abide here henceforth, this shall be the sod of my death." And I made a vow to live in this little cloister alone, or with a few pupils, I who had been restless and a wanderer, and a seeker after difficult things; the King will not grudge me the loneliness of my cloister.

THE MESSENGER. I will say all this to the King. These lads will come with me?

CIARAN. Will ye go to the King's feast, lads?

BREASAL. May we go, Master.

CIARAN. I will not gainsay you.

MAINE. It will be a great thing to sit at the King's table.

CEALLACH. Master, it may turn aside the King's displeasure for your not going if we go in your name. We may, perchance, bring the King here, and peace will be bound between you.

CIARAN. May God be near you in the places to which you go.

CEALLACH. I am loath to leave you alone, Master.

CIARAN. Little Iollann will stay with me. Will you not, little Iollann.

Iollann Beag looks yearningly towards the Messenger and the others as if he would fain go; then he turns to Ciaran.

IOLLANN BEAG. I will.

CIARAN (*caressing him*). That is my good little lad.

ART. We will bring you back some of the King's mead, Iollann.

IOLLANN BEAG. Bring me some of his apples and his hazel-nuts.

RONAN. We will, and, maybe, a roast capon, or a piece of venison.

They all go out laughing. Ceallach turns back in the door.

CEALLACH. Good-bye, Master.

CIARAN. May you go safe, lad. (*To Iollann*). You are my whole school now, Iollann.

IOLLANN (*sitting down at his knee*). Do you think the King will come here?

CIARAN. Yes, I think he will come.

IOLLANN. I would like to see him. Is he a great, tall man?

CIARAN. I have not seen him for a long time; not since he and I were lads.

IOLLANN. Were you friends?

CIARAN. We were fostered together.

IOLLANN. Is he a wicked King?

CIARAN. No; he has ruled this country well. His people love him. They have gone into many perilous places with him, and he has never failed them.

IOLLANN. Why then does he hate you? Why do Ceallach and the others fear that he may do you harm?

CIARAN. For twenty years Daire and I have stood over against each other. When we were at school we were rivals for the first place. I was first in all manly games; Daire was first in learning. Everyone said "Ciaran will be a great warrior and Daire will be a great poet or a great teacher." And yet it has not been so. I was nearly as good as he in learning, and he was nearly as good as I in manly feats. I said that I would be his master in all things, and he said that he would be my master. And we strove one against the other.

IOLLANN BEAG. Why did you want to be his master?

CIARAN. I do not know. I thought that I should be happy if I were first and Daire

86

only second. But Daire was always first.
I sought out difficult things to do that I
might become a better man than he : I went
into far countries and won renown among
strange peoples, but very little wealth and
no happiness ; I sailed into seas that no man
before me had sailed into, and saw islands
that only God and the angels had seen
before me ; I learned outland tongues and
read the books of many peoples and their
old lore ; and when I came back to my own
country I found that Daire was its king,
and that all men loved him. Me they had
forgotten.

IOLLANN BEAG. Were you sad when you
came home and found that you were forgotten?

CIARAN. No, I was glad. I said, "This
is a hard thing that I have found to do, to
live lonely and unbeloved among my own
kin. Daire has not done anything as hard as
this." In one of the cities that I had sailed
to I had heard of the true, illustrious God,
and of men who had gone out from warm
and pleasant houses, and from the kindly
faces of neighbours to live in desert places,
where God walked alone and terrible ; and
I said that I would do that hard thing,

though I would fain have stayed in my father's house. And so I came into this wilderness, where I have lived for seven years. For a few years I was alone; then pupils began to come to me. By-and-bye the druids gave out word that I was teaching new things and breaking established custom; and the King has forbade my teaching, and I have not desisted, and so he and I stand opposed as of old.

IOLLANN BEAG. You will win this time, little Master.

CIARAN. I think so; I hope so, dear. (*Aside.*) I would I could say " I know so." This seems to me the hardest thing I have tried to do. Can a soldier fight for a cause of which he is not sure? Can a teacher die for a thing he does not believe? . . . Forgive me, Lord! It is my weakness that cries out. I believe, I believe; help my unbelief. (*To Iollann Beag.*) Why do you think I shall win this time, Iollann,—I who have always lost?

IOLLANN BEAG. Because God's great angels will fight for you. Will they not?

CIARAN. Yes, I think they will. All that old chivalry stands harnessed in Heaven.

88

IOLLANN BEAG. Will they not come if you call them?

CIARAN. Yes, they will come. (*Aside.*) Is it a true thing I tell this child or do I lie to him? Will they come at my call? Will they come at my call? My spirit reaches out and finds Heaven empty. The great halls stand horseless and riderless. I have called to you, O riders, and I have not heard the thunder of your coming. The multitudinous, many-voiced sea and the green, quiet earth have each its children, but where are the sons of Heaven? Where in all this temple of the world, this dim and wondrous temple, does its God lurk?

IOLLANN BEAG. And would they come if I were to call them—old Peter, and the Baptist John, and Michael and his riders?

CIARAN. We are taught that if one calls them with faith they will come.

IOLLANN BEAG. Could I see them and speak to them?

CIARAN. If it were necessary for any dear purpose of God's, as to save a soul that were in peril, we are taught that they would come in bodily presence, and that one could see them and speak to them.

IOLLANN BEAG. If the soul of any dear friend of mine be ever in peril I will call upon them. I will say, "Baptist John, Baptist John, attend him. Good Peter of the Sword, strike valiantly. Young Michael, stand near with all the heroes of Heaven!"

CIARAN (*aside*). If the soul of any dear friend of his were in peril! The peril is near! The peril is near!

A knock at the postern; Iollann Beag looks towards Ciaran.

CIARAN. Run, Iollann, and see who knocks. (*Iollann Beag goes out.*) I have looked back over the journey of my life as a man at evening might look back from a hill on the roads he had travelled since morning. I have seen with a great clearness as if I had left this green, dim wood and climbed to the top of that far hill I have seen from me for seven years now, yet never climbed. And I see that all my wayfaring has been in vain. A man may not escape from that which is in himself. A man shall not find his quest unless he kill the dearest thing he has. I thought that I was sacrificing everything, but I have not sacrificed the old pride of my heart. I chose self-abnegation, not out of humility, but out of pride: and God, that terrible hidden God, has punished me by withholding from me His most precious gift of faith. Faith comes to the humble only. . . . Nay, Lord, I believe: this is but a temptation. Thou, too, wast tempted. Thou, too, wast forsaken. O valiant Christ, give me Thy strength! My need is great. *Iollann Beag returns.*

IOLLANN BEAG. There is a warrior at the door, Master, that asks a shelter. He says he has lost his way in the wood.

CIARAN. Bid him to come in Iollann. (*Iollann Beag goes to the door again.*) I, too, have lost my way. I am like one that has trodden intricate forest paths that have crossed and recrossed and never led him to any homestead; or like a mariner that has voyaged on a shoreless sea yearning for a glimpse of green earth, yet never descrying it. If I could find some little place to rest, if I could but lie still at last after so much wayfaring, after such clamour of loud-voiced winds, methinks that would be to find God; for is not God quiet, is not God peace? But always I go on with a cry as of baying winds or of vociferous hounds about me. . . . They say the King hunts me to-day: but the King is not so terrible a hunter as the desires and the doubts of a man's heart. The King I can meet unafraid, but who is not afraid of himself? (*Daire enters, wrapped in a long mantle, and stands a little within the threshold: Iollann Beag behind him. Ciaran looks fixedly at him; then speaks.*) You have hunted well to-day, O Daire !

DAIRE. I am famed as a hunter.

CIARAN. When I was a young man I said, " I will strive with the great untamed elements, with the ancient, illimitable sea and the anarchic winds ; " you, in the manner of Kings, have warred with timid, furtive creatures, and it has taught you only cruelty and craft.

DAIRE. What has your warfare taught you ? I do not find you changed, Ciaran. Your old pride but speaks a new language. . . . I am, as you remind me, only a King ; but I have been a good King. Have you been a good teacher?

CIARAN. My pupils must answer.

DAIRE. Where are your pupils?

CIARAN. True ; they are not here.

92

DAIRE. They are at an ale-feast in my
tent. . . . (*Coming nearer to Ciaran.*)
I have not come to taunt you, Ciaran.
Nor should you taunt me. You seem to
me to have spent your life pursuing shadows
that fled before you ; yea, pursuing ghosts
over wide spaces and through the devious
places of the world : and I pity you for the
noble manhood you have wasted. I seem
to you to have spent my life busy with the
little, vulgar tasks and the little, vulgar
pleasures of a King : and you pity me because
I have not adventured, because I have not
been tried, because I have not suffered as
you have. It should be sufficient triumph
for each of us that each pities the other.

CIARAN. You speak gently, Daire ; and
you speak wisely. You were always wise.
And yet, methinks, you are wrong. There
is a deeper antagonism between you and me
than you are aware of. It is not merely
that the little things about you, the little,
foolish, mean, discordant things of a man's
life, have satisfied you, and that I have been
discontent, seeking things remote and holy
and perilous —

DAIRE. Ghosts, ghosts !

CIARAN. Nay, they alone are real; or, rather, it alone is real. For though its names be many, its substance is one. One man will call it happiness, another will call it beauty, a third will call it holiness, a fourth will call it rest. I have sought it under all its names.

DAIRE. What is it that you have sought?

CIARAN. I have sought truth.

DAIRE. And have you found truth? (*Ciaran bows his head in dejection.*) Ciaran, was it worth your while to give up all goodly life to follow that mocking phantom? I do not say that a man should not renounce ease. I have not loved ease. But I have loved power, and victory, and life, and men, and women, and the gracious sun. He who renounces these things to follow a phantom across a world has given his all for nothing.

CIARAN. Is not the mere quest often worth while, even if the thing quested be never found?

DAIRE. And so you have not found your quest?

CIARAN. You lay subtle traps for me in your speeches, Daire. It was your way at school when we disputed.

94

DAIRE. Kings must be subtle. It is by craft we rule. . . . Ciaran, for the shadow you have pursued I offer you a substance; in place of vain journeying I invite you to rest. . . . If you make your peace with me you shall be the second man in my kingdom.

CIARAN (*in scorn and wrath*). The second man!

DAIRE. There speaks your old self, Ciaran. I did not mean to wound you. I am the King, chosen by the people to rule and lead. I could not, even if I would, place you above me; but I will place you at my right hand.

CIARAN. You would bribe me with this petty honour?

DAIRE. No. I would gain you for the service of your people. What other service should a man take upon him?

CIARAN. I told you that you did not understand the difference between you and me. May one not serve the people by bearing testimony in their midst to a true thing even as by feeding them with bread?

DAIRE. Again you prate of truth. Are you fond enough to think that what has not imposed even upon your pupils will impose upon me?

CIARAN. My pupils believe. You must not wrong them, Daire.

DAIRE. Are you sure of them?

CIARAN. Yes, I am sure. (*Aside.*) Yet sometimes I thought that that gibing Maine did not believe. It may be —

DAIRE. Where are your pupils? Why are they not here to stand by you in your bitter need?

CIARAN. You enticed them from me by guile.

DAIRE. I invited them; they came. You could not keep them, Ciaran. Think you my young men would have left me, in similar case? Their bodies would have been my bulwark against a host.

CIARAN. You hint unspeakable things.

DAIRE. I do but remind you that you have to-day no disciples; (*smiling*) except, perhaps, this little lad. Come, I will win him from you with an apple.

CIARAN. You shall not tempt him!

DAIRE (*laughing*). Ciaran, you stand confessed: you have no faith in your disciples; methinks you have no faith in your religion.

96

CIARAN. You are cruel, Daire. You were not so cruel when we were lads.

DAIRE. You have come into my country preaching to my people new things, incredible things, things you dare not believe yourself. I will not have this lie preached to men. If your religion be true, you must give me a sign of its truth.

CIARAN. It is true, it is true!

DAIRE. Give me a sign. Nay, show me that you yourself believe. Call upon your God to reveal Himself. I do not trust these skulking gods.

CIARAN. Who am I to ask that great Mystery to unveil Its face? Who are you that a miracle should be wrought for you?

DAIRE. This is not an answer. So priests ever defend their mysteries. I will not be put off as one would put off a child that asks questions. Lo, here I bare my sword against God; lo, here I lift up my shield. Let one of his great captains come down to answer the challenge!

CIARAN. This the bragging of a fool.

DAIRE. Nor does that answer me. Ciaran, you are in my power. My young men surround this house. Yours are at an ale-feast.

CIARAN. O wise and far-seeing King! You have planned all well.

DAIRE. There is a watcher at every door of your house. There a tracker on every path of the forest. The wild boar crouches in his lair for fear of the men that fill this wood. Three rings of champions ring round the tent in which your pupils feast. Your God had need to show Himself a God!

CIARAN. Nay, slay me, Daire. I will bear testimony with my life.

DAIRE. What will that prove? Men die for false things, for ridiculous things, for evil things. What vile cause has not its heroes? Though you were to die here with joy and laughter you would not prove your cause a true one. Ciaran, let God send down an angel to stand between you and me.

CIARAN. Do you think that to save my poor life Omnipotence will display Itself?

DAIRE. Who talks of your life? It is your soul that is at stake, and mine, and this little boy's, and the souls of all this nation, born and unborn.

CIARAN (*aside*). He speaks true.

DAIRE. Nay, I will put you to the proof.
(*To Iollann.*) Come hither, child. (*Iollann
Beag approaches.*) He is daintily fashioned,
Ciaran, this last little pupil of yours. I
swear to you that he shall die unless your
God sends down an angel to rescue him.
Kneel boy. (*Iollann Beag kneels.*) Speak
now, if God has ears to hear.

He raises his sword.

CIARAN (*aside*). I dare not speak. My
God, my God, why hast Thou forsaken me?

IOLLANN BEAG. Fear not, little Master, I
remember the word you taught me. . . .
Young Michael, stand near me!

*The figure of a mighty Warrior, winged,
and clothed in light, seems to stand beside the
boy. Ciaran bends on one knee.*

DAIRE. Who art thou, O Soldier?

MICHAEL. I am he that waiteth at the
portal. I am he that hasteneth. I am he that
rideth before the squadron. I am he that
holdeth a shield over the retreat of man's
host when Satan cometh in war. I am he
that turneth and smiteth. I am he that is
Captain of the Host of God.

Daire bends slowly on one knee.

IOSAGAN

SCENE I

A sea-strand beside a village in Iar-Connacht. A house on the right-hand side. The sound of a bell comes east, very clearly. The door of the house is opened. An aged man, old Matthias, comes out on the door-flag and stands for a spell looking down the road. He sits then on a chair that is outside the door, his two hands gripping a stick, his head bent, and he listening attentively to the sound of the bell. The bell stops ringing. Daragh, Padraic and Coilin come up from the sea and they putting on their share of clothes after bathing.

DARAGH (*stretching his finger towards the sea*). The flowers are white in the fisherman's garden.

PADRAIC. They are, *muise*.

COILIN. Where are they?

DARAGH. See them out on the sea.

COILIN. Those are not white flowers. Those are white horses.

DARAGH. They're like white flowers.

COILIN. No; Old Matthias says those are the white horses that go galloping across the sea from the Other Country.

PADRAIC. I heard Iosagan saying they were flowers.

COILIN. What way would flowers grow on the sea?

PADRAIC. And what way would horses travel on the sea?

COILIN. Easy, if they were fairy horses would be in them.

PADRAIC. And wouldn't flowers grow on the sea as easy, if they were fairy flowers would be in them? Isn't it often you saw the water-lilies on Loch Ellery? And couldn't they grow on the sea as well as on the lake?

COILIN. I don't know if they could.

PADRAIC. They could, *muise*.

DARAGH. The sea was fine to-day, lad.

COILIN. It was, but it was devilish cold.

PADRAIC. Why wouldn't you be cold when you'd only go into your knees?

COILIN. By my word, I was afraid the waves would knock me down if I'd go in any further. They were terrible big.

DARAGH. That's what I like, lad. Do you mind yon terrible big one that came over our heads?

PADRAIC. Aye, and Coilin screaming out he was drowned.

COILIN. It went down my throat; it did that, and it nearly smothered me.

PADRAIC. Sure, you had your mouth open, and you shouting. It would be a queer story if it didn't go down your throat.

COILIN, Yon one gave me enough. I kept out of their way after that.

DARAGH. Have the other lads on them yet?

PADRAIC. Aye. Here they are.

COILIN. Look at Feichin's hair!

Feichin, Eoghan and Cuimin come up from the sea and they drying their hair.

CUIMIN. What'll we play to-day?

COILIN. "Blind Man's Buff!"

PADRAIC. Ara, shut up, yourself and your "Blind Man's Buff."

COILIN. "High Gates," then!

PADRAIC. No. We're tired of those "High Gates."

DARAGH. Has anybody a ball?

CUIMIN. And if they had, itself, where would we play?

PADRAIC. Against Old Matthias's gable-end. There's no nicer place to be found.

COILIN. Who has the ball?

CUIMIN. My soul, I haven't it.

DARAGH. No, nor I.

PADRAIC. You yourself, Coilin, had it on Friday.

COILIN. By my word, didn't the master grab it where I was hopping it in the school at Catechism?

FEICHIN. True for you, lad.

CUIMIN. My soul, but I thought he'd give you the rod that time.

COILIN. He would, too, only he was expecting the priest to come in.

DARAGH. It's the ball he wanted. He'll have a game with the peelers to-day after Mass.

PADRAIC. My soul, but he will, and it's he can beat the peelers, too.

DARAGH. He can't beat the sergeant. The sergeant's the best man of them all. He beat Hoskins and the red man together last Sunday.

FEICHIN. Ara, stop! Did he beat them?

DARAGH. He did, *muise*. The red man was raging, and the master and the peelers all laughing at him.

PADRAIC. I bet the master will beat the sergeant.

DARAGH. I'll bet he won't.

PADRAIC. Do ye hear him?

DARAGH. I'll bet the sergeant can beat any man in this country.

PADRAIC. Ara, how do you know whether he can or not?

DARAGH. I know well he can. Don't I be always watching them?

PADRAIC. You don't know!

DARAGH. I do know! It's I that know it!

They threaten each other. A quarrel arises among the boys, a share of them saying, "The sergeant's the best!" and others, "The master's best!" Old Matthias gets up to listen to them. He comes forward, twisted and bent in his body, and barely able to drag his feet along. He speaks to them quietly, laying his hand on Daragh's head.

MATTHIAS. O! O! O! My shame ye are!

PADRAIC. This fellow says the master can't beat the sergeant playing ball.

DARAGH. By my word, wouldn't the sergeant beat anybody at all in this country, Matthias?

MATTHIAS. Never mind the sergeant. Look at that lonesome wild goose that's making on us over Loch Ellery! Look!

All the boys look up.

PADRAIC. I see it, by my soul!

DARAGH. Where's she coming from, Matthias?

MATTHIAS. From the Eastern World. I would say she has travelled a thousand miles since she left her nest in the lands to the north.

COILIN. The poor thing. And where will she drop?

MATTHIAS. To Aran she'll go, it's a chance. See her now out over the sea. My love you are, lonesome wild goose!

COILIN. Tell us a story, Matthias.

He sits on a stone by the strand-edge, and the boys gather round him.

MATTHIAS. What story shall I tell?

FEICHIN. "The Adventures of the Grey Horse!"

CUIMIN. "The Hen-Harrier and the Wren!"

PADRAIC. "The Two-Headed Giant!"

COILIN. "The Adventures of the Piper in the Snail's Castle!"

EOGHAN. Aye, by my soul, "The Adventures of the Piper in the Snail's Castle!"

THE BOYS (*with one voice*). "The Adventures of the Piper in the Snail's Castle!"

MATTHIAS. I'll do that. "There was a Snail in it long ago, and it's long since it was. If we'd been there that time, we wouldn't be here now; and if we were, itself, we'd have a new story or an old story, and that's better than to be without e'er a story at all. The Castle this Snail lived in was the finest that man's eye ever saw. It was greater entirely, and it was a thousand times richer than Meave's Castle in Rath Cruachan, or than the Castle of the High-King of Ireland itself in Tara of the Kings. This Snail made love to a Spider —"

COILIN. No, Matthias, wasn't it to a Granny's Needle he made love?

MATTHIAS. My soul, but you're right. What's coming on me?

PADRAIC. Go on, Matthias.

MATTHIAS. "This Nettle-Worm was very comely entirely —"

FEICHIN. What's the Nettle-Worm, Matthias ?

MATTHIAS. Why, the Nettle-Worm he made love to.

CUIMIN. But I thought it was to a Granny's Needle he made love.

MATTHIAS. Was it ? The story's going from me. "This Piper was in love with the daughter of the King of Connacht —"

EOGHAN. But you didn't mention the Piper yet, Matthias !

MATTHIAS. Didn't I ! "The Piper . . . " yes, by my soul, the Piper — I'm losing my memory. Look here, neighbours, we won't meddle with the story to-day. Let's have a song.

COILIN. "Hi diddle dum!"

MATTHIAS. Are ye satisfied ?

THE BOYS. We are.

MATTHIAS. I'll do that. (*He sings the following rhyme*) :

"Hi diddle dum, the cat and his
      mother,
That went to Galway riding a drake."

THE BOYS. And hi diddle dum !

MATTHIAS.

" Hi diddle dum, the rain came pelting,
And drenched to the skin the cat and his
mother."

THE BOYS. And hi diddle dum !

MATTHIAS.

" Hi diddle dum, 'twas like in the deluge
The cat and his mother would both be
drownded."

THE BOYS. And hi diddle dum !

MATTHIAS.

" Hi diddle dum, my jewel the drake was,
That carried his burden — "

COILIN. Swimming —

MATTHIAS. Good man, Coilin.

" That carried his burden swimming to
Galway."

THE BOYS. And hi diddle dum !

*Old Matthias shakes his head wearily ;
he speaks in a sad voice.*

MATTHIAS. My songs are going from
me, neighbours. I'm like an old fiddle
that's lost all its strings.

CUIMIN. Haven't you the " *Báidín* "
always, Matthias ?

MATTHIAS. I have, my soul; I have it
as long as I'm living. I won't lose the

" *Báidín* " till I'm stretched in the clay.
Shall we have it ?

THE BOYS. Aye.

MATTHIAS. Are ye ready to go rowing ?

THE BOYS. We are !

*They order themselves as they would be
rowing. Old Matthias sings these verses.*

MATTHIAS.

" I will hang a sail, and I will go west."

THE BOYS. *Oró, mo churaichín, O !*

MATTHIAS.

" And till St. John's Day I will not rest."

THE BOYS. *Oró, mo churaichín, O !*
Oró, mo churaichín. O !
'S óró, mo bháidín !

MATTHIAS.

" Isn't it fine, my little boat, sailing on the
bay."

THE BOYS. *Oró, mo churaichín, O !*

MATTHIAS. "The oars pulling —"

*He stops suddenly, and puts his hand to
his head.*

PADRAIC. What's on you, Matthias ?

EOGHAN. Are you sick, Matthias ?

MATTHIAS. Something that came on my
head. It's nothing. What's this I was
saying ?

COILIN. You were saying the "*Báidín*," Matthias, but don't mind if you don't feel well. Are you sick ?

MATTHIAS. Sick ? By my word, I'm not sick. What would make me sick ? We'll start again :

"Isn't it fine, my little boat, sailing on the bay."

THE BOYS. *Oró, mo churaichín, O !*

MATTHIAS. "The oars pulling strongly—" (*He stops again.*) Neighbours, the "*Báidín*" itself is gone from me. (*They remain silent for a spell, the old man sitting and his head bent on his breast, and the boys looking on him sorrowfully. The old man speaks with a start.*) Are those the people coming home from Mass ?

CUIMIN. No. They won't be free for a half hour yet.

COILIN. Why don't you go to Mass, Matthias ?

The old man rises up and puts his hand to his head again. He speaks angrily at first, and after that softly.

MATTHIAS. Why don't I go ? . . . I'm not good enough. By my word, God

114

wouldn't hear me. . . . What's this I'm saying? . . . (*He laughs.*) And I have lost the "*Báidín*," do ye say? Amn't I the pitiful object without my "*Báidín!*"

He hobbles slowly across the road. Coilin rises and puts his shoulder under the old man's hand to support him. The boys begin playing "jackstones" quietly. Old Matthias sits on the chair again, and Coilin returns. Daragh speaks in a low voice.

DARAGH. There's something on Old Matthias to-day. He never forgot the "*Báidín*" before.

CUIMIN. I heard my father saying to my mother, the other night, that it's not long he has to live.

COILIN. Do you think is he very old?

PADRAIC. Why did you put that question on him about the Mass? Don't you know he hasn't been seen at Mass in the memory of the people?

DARAGH. I heard Old Cuimin Enda saying to my father that he himself saw Old Matthias at Mass when he was a youth.

COILIN. Do you know why he doesn't go to Mass now?

PADRAIC (*in a whisper*). It's said he doesn't believe there's a God.

CUIMIN. I heard Father Sean Eamonn saying it's the way he did some terrible sin at the start of his life, and when the priest wouldn't give him absolution in confession there came a raging anger on him, and he swore an oath he wouldn't touch priest or chapel for ever again.

DARAGH. That's not how I heard it. One night when I was in bed the old people were talking and whispering by the fireside, and I heard Maire of the Bridge saying to the other old women that it's the way Matthias sold his soul to some Great Man he met once on the top of Cnoc-a'-Daimh, and that this Man wouldn't allow him to go to Mass.

PADRAIC. Do you think was it the devil he saw?

DARAGH. I don't know. A " Great Man," said Maire of the Bridge.

CUIMIN. I wouldn't believe a word of it. Sure, if Matthias sold his soul to the devil it must be he's a wicked person.

PADRAIC. He's not a wicked person, *muise*. Don't you mind the day Iosagan said that his father told him Matthias would be among the saints on the Day of the Mountain ?

CUIMIN. I mind it well.

COILIN. Where's Iosagan from us to-day?

DARAGH. He never comes when there does be a grown person watching us.

CUIMIN. Wasn't he here a week ago to-day when old Matthias was watching us?

DARAGH. Was he?

CUIMIN. He was.

PADRAIC. Aye, and a fortnight to-day, as well.

DARAGH. There's a chance he'll come to-day, then.   *Cuimin rises and looks east.*

CUIMIN. O, see, he's coming.

Iosagan enters—a little, brown-haired boy, a white coat on him, and he without shoes or cap like the other boys. The boys welcome him.

THE BOYS. God save you, Iosagan !

IOSAGAN. God and Mary save you !

He sits among them, a hand of his about Daragh's neck; the boys begin playing again, gently, without noise or quarrelling. Iosagan joins in the game. Matthias rises with a start on the coming of Iosagan, and stands

117

gazing at him. After they have played for a spell he comes towards them, and then stands again and calls over to Coilin.

MATTHIAS. Coilin!

COILIN. What do you want?

MATTHIAS. Come here to me. (*Coilin rises and goes to him.*) Who is that boy I see among you this fortnight back—he, yonder, with the brown head on him—but take care it's not red he is; I don't know is it black or is it fair he is, the way the sun is burning on him? Do you see him—him that has his arm about Daragh's neck?

COILIN. That's Iosagan.

MATTHIAS. Iosagan?

COILIN. That's the name he gives himself.

MATTHIAS. Who are his people?

COILIN. I don't know, but he says his father's a king.

MATTHIAS. Where does he live?

COILIN. He never told us that, but he says his house isn't far away.

MATTHIAS. Does he be among you often?

COILIN. He does, when we do be amusing ourselves like this. But he goes from us when grown people come near. He will

go from us now as soon as the people begin
coming from Mass.

*The boys rise and go, in ones and twos,
when they have finished the game.*

COILIN. O! They are going jumping.

*He runs out after the others. Iosagan
and Daragh rise and go. Matthias comes
forward and calls Iosagan.*

MATTHIAS. Iosagan! (*The Child turns
back and comes towards him at a run.*) Come
here and sit on my knee for a little while,
Iosagan. (*The Child links his hand in the old
man's hand, and they cross the road together.
Matthias sits on his chair and draws Iosagan to
him.*) Where do you live, Iosagan?

IOSAGAN. Not far from this my house is.
Why don't you come to see me?

MATTHIAS. I would be afraid in a royal
house. They tell me that your father's a
king.

IOSAGAN. He is High-King of the World.
But there's no call for you to be afraid of
Him. He's full of pity and love.

MATTHIAS. I fear I didn't keep His law.

IOSAGAN. Ask forgiveness of Him. I and
my Mother will make intercession for you.

MATTHIAS. It's a pity I didn't see You

before this, Iosagan. Where were You
from me?

IOSAGAN. I was here always. I do be
travelling the roads and walking the hills
and ploughing the waves. I do be among
the people when they gather into My house.
I do be among the children they do leave
behind them playing on the street.

MATTHIAS. I was too shy, or too proud,
to go into Your house, Iosagan : among the
children, it was, I found You.

IOSAGAN. There isn't any place or time
the children do be making fun to themselves
that I'm not with them. Times they see
Me ; other times they don't see Me.

MATTHIAS. I never saw You till lately.

IOSAGAN. All the grown people do be
blind.

MATTHIAS. And it has been granted me
to see You, Iosagan.

IOSAGAN. My Father gave Me leave to
show Myself to you because you loved His
little children. (*The voices are heard of the
people returning from Mass.*) I must go now
from you.

MATTHIAS. Let me kiss the hem of
Your coat.

PRIEST. A mannerly little boy, with a white coat on him.

MATTHIAS. Did you take notice if there was a shadow of light about his head?

PRIEST. I did, and it put great wonder on me.

The door opens. Iosagan stands on the threshold, and He with His two arms stretched out towards Matthias; a miraculous light about His face and head.

MATTHIAS. Iosagan! You're good, Iosagan. You didn't fail me, love. I was too proud to go into Your house, but at the last it was granted me to see You. " I was here always," says He. " I do be travelling the roads and walking the hills and ploughing the waves. I do be among the people when they gather into My house. I do be among the children they do leave behind playing on the street." Among the children, it was, I found You, Iosagan. " Shall I see You again?" " You will," says He. "You'll see Me to-night." *Sé do bheatha, a Iosagáin!*

He falls back on the bed, and he dead. The Priest goes softly to him and closes his eves.

CURTAIN

THE MOTHER

There was a company of women sitting up one night in the house of Barbara of the Bridge, spinning frieze. It would be music to you to be listening to them, and their voices making harmony with the drone of the wheels, like the sound of the wind with the shaking of the bushes.

They heard a cry. The child, it was, talking in its sleep.

"Some evil thing that crossed the door," says Barbara. "Rise, Maire, and stir the cradle."

The woman spoken-to got up. She was sitting on the floor till that, carding. She went over to the cradle. The child was wide awake before her, and he crying pitifully. Maire knelt down beside the cradle. As soon as the child saw her face he ceased from crying. A long, beautiful face she had; a brow, broad and smooth, black hair and it twisted in clusters about her head, and two grey eyes that would look on you slow, serious, and troubled-like.

It was a gift Maire had, the way she would quieten a cross child or put a sick child to sleep, looking on that smooth, pleasant face and those grey, loving eyes of hers.

Maire began singing the "*Crónán na Banaltra*" (The Nurse's Lullaby) in a low voice. The other women ceased from their talk to listen to her. It wasn't long till the child was in a dead sleep. Maire rose and went back to where she was sitting before. She fell to her carding again.

"May you have good, Maire," says Barbara. "There's no wonder in life but the way you're able to put children asleep. Though that's my own heir, I would be hours of the clock with him before he would go off on me."

"Maire has magic," says another woman.

"She's like the harpers of Meave that would put a host of men asleep when they would play their sleep-tunes," says old Una ní Greelis.

"Isn't it fine she can sing the *Crónán na Banaltra?*" says the second woman.

"My soul, you would think it was the Virgin herself that would be saying it," says old Una.

"Do you think is it true, Una, that it was the Blessed Virgin (praise to her for ever) that made that tune?" says Barbara.

"I know it's true. Isn't it with that tune she used put the Son of God (a thousand glories to His name) asleep when He was a child?"

"And how is it, then, the people do have it now?" says Barbara.

"Coming down from generation to generation, I suppose, like the Fenian tales," says one of the women.

"No, my soul," says old Una. "The people it was heard the tune from the Virgin's mouth itself, here in this countryside, not so long ago."

"And how would they hear it?"

"Doesn't the world know that the glorious Virgin goes round the townlands every Christmas Eve, herself and her child?"

"I heard the people saying she does."

"And don't you know if the door is left ajar and a candle lighting in the window, that the Virgin and her Child will come into the house, and that they will sit down to rest themselves?"

"My soul, but I heard that, too."

"A woman of the Joyce country, it was, waiting up on Christmas Eve to see the Virgin, that heard the tune from her for the first time and taught it to the country. It's often I heard discourse about her, and I a growing girl. 'Maire of the Virgin' was the name they gave her. It's said that it's often she saw the glorious Virgin. She died in the poorhouse in Uachtar Ard a couple of years before I was married. The blessing of God be with the souls of the dead."

"Amen, O Lord," say the other women.

But Maire did not speak. She and her two big grey eyes were going, as you would say, through old Una's forehead, and she telling the story. She spoke after a spell.

"Are you sure, Una, that the Virgin and her Child come into the houses on Christmas Eve ?" says she.

"As sure as I'm living."

"Did you ever see her ?"

"I did not, then. But the Christmas Eve after I was married I waited up to see her, if it would be granted me. A cloud of sleep fell on me. Some noise woke me, and when I opened my eyes I thought

130

I saw, as it would be, a young woman and a child in her arms going out the door."

No one spoke for a long time. Nothing was heard in the house but the drone of the spinning-wheels and the crackling of the fire, and the chirping of the crickets. Maire got up.

" I'll be shortening the road," says she. " May God give you good night, women."

"God speed you, Maire," they answered together.

She drew-to the door on herself.

There was, as it would be, a blaze of fire in that woman's heart, and she going the road home in the blackness of night. The great longing of her soul was plundering and desolating her—the longing for children. She had been married four years, and hadn't clann. It's often she would spend the hours on her knees, praying God to send her a child. It's often she would rise from the bed in the night-time, and go on her two naked knees on the cold, hard stone making the same petition. It's many a penance she used put on herself in hopes that the torture of her body would soften God's heart. It's often when her man would be

131

from home, that she would go to sleep
without dinner and without supper. Once
or twice, when her man was asleep, she left
the bed and went out and stood a long while
under the dew of the night sending her
prayer to the dark, lonesome skies. Once
she drew blood from her shoulder-blades
with blows she gave herself with a switch.
Another time she stuck thorns into her flesh
in memory of the crown of thorns that went
on the brow of the Saviour. The penances
and the heart-scald were preying on her
health. Nobody guessed what was wrong
with her. Her own husband—a decent,
kindly man—didn't understand the story
right, though it's often he would hear her
in the night talking to herself as a mother
would be talking to a child, when she would
feel its hand or its mouth at her breast. Ah!
it's many a woman hugs her heart and
whispers in the dead time of night to the
child that isn't born, and will not be.

Maire thought long until Christmas Eve
came. But as there's a wearing on everything, so there was a wearing on the delay
of that time. The day of Christmas Eve
was tedious to her until evening came. She

swept the floor of the house, and she cleaned the chairs, and she made up a good fire before going to sleep. She left the door on the latch, and she put a tall, white candle in the window. When she stretched herself beside her man it wasn't to sleep it was, but to watch. She thought her man would never sleep. She felt at last by the quiet breath he was drawing that he was gone off. Then she got up. She put on her dress, and she stole out to the kitchen. No one was there. Not even a mouse was stirring. The crickets themselves were asleep. The fire was in red ashes. The candle was shining brightly. She bent on her knees in the room door. It's sweet the calm of the house was to her in the middle of the night, though, I tell you, it was terrible. There came a heightening of mind on her as it used to come betimes in the chapel, and she going to receive communion from the priest's hands. She felt, somehow, that the Presence wasn't far from her, and that it wouldn't be long until she would hear a footstep. She listened patiently. The house itself, she thought, and what was in it both living and dead, was listening as well. The hills were listening, and the stones of the earth, and the starry stars of the sky.

She heard a sound. A footstep on the door-flag. She saw a young woman coming in and a child in her arms. The young woman drew up to the fire. She sat down on a chair. She began crooning, very low, to the child. Maire recognised the music. The tune that was on it was the " *Crónán na Banaltra.*"

A while to them like that. The woman hugging the child to her breast, and crooning, very sweetly, very softly. Maire on her two knees, under the shadow of the door. It wasn't in her to speak nor to move. She was barely able to draw her breath.

At last the woman rose. It's then Maire rose. She went hither to the woman.

" *A Mhuire,*" says she, whispering-like.

The woman turned her countenance towards her. A lovely, noble countenance it was.

" *A Mhuire,*" says Maire again. "I have a request of you."

" Say it," says the other woman.

" A child drinking the milk of my breast," says Maire. "Don't deny me, *a Mhuire.*"

134

"Come closer to me," says the other woman.

Maire came closer to her. The other woman raised her child. The child stretched out its two little hands, and it laid a hand softly on each cheek of Maire's two cheeks.

"That blessing will make you fruitful," says the Mother.

"Its a good woman you are, *a Mhuire*," says Maire. "It's good your Son is."

"I leave a blessing in this house," says the other woman.

She squeezed her child to her breast again and went out the door. Maire fell on her knees.

.   .   .   .

It's a year since that Christmas Eve. The last time I passed Maire's house there was a child in her breast. There was that look on her that doesn't be on living soul but a mother when she feels the mouth of her firstborn at her nipple.

"God loves the women better than the men," said I to myself. "It's to them He sends the greatest sorrows, and it's on them He bestows the greatest joy."

135

THE DEARG-DAOL

A walking-man, it was, come into my
father's house out of the Joyce Country,
that told us this story by the fireside one
wild winter's night. The wind was wailing
round the house, like women keening the
dead, while he spoke, and he would make
his voice rise or fall according as the wind's
voice would rise or fall. A tall man he was,
with wild eyes, and his share of clothes
almost in tatters. There was a sort of fear
on me of him when he came in, and his
story didn't lessen my fear.

The three most blessed beasts in the world,
says the walking-man, are the haddock, the
robin redbreast, and God's cow. And the
three most cursed beasts in the world are
the viper, the wren, and the *dearg-daol*
("black chafer"). And it's the *dearg-daol*
is the most cursed of them. 'Tis I that
know that. Woman of the house, if a man
would murder his son, don't call him the
dearg-daol. If a woman would come between
yourself and the husband of your bed, don't
put her in comparison with the *dearg-daol*.

" God save us," says my mother.

" Amen, Lord," says the walking-man.

He didn't speak again for a spell. We all listened, for we knew he was going to tell a story. It wasn't long before he began.

When I was a lad, says the walking-man, there was a woman of our people that everybody was afraid of. In a little, lonely cabin in a gap of a mountain, it was, she lived. No one would go near her house. She, herself, wouldn't come next or near any other body's house. Nobody would speak to her when they met her on the road. She wouldn't put word nor wisdom on anybody at all. You'd think a pity to see the creature and she going the road alone.

" Who is she," I would say to my mother, " or why wouldn't they speak to her ? "

" Whisht, boy," my mother would say to me. " That's the *Dearg-Daol.* 'Tis a cursed woman she is."

" What did she do, or who put the curse on her ? " I would say.

" A priest of God that put the curse on her," my mother would say. " No one in life knew what she did."

And that's all the knowledge I got of

her until I was a grown chap. And indeed
to you, neighbours, I never heard anything
about her but that she committed some
dreadful sin at the start of her life, and that
the priest put his curse on her before the
people on account of that sin. One
Sunday, when the people were gathered at
Mass, the priest turned round on them, and
says he :—

" There is a woman here," says he, " that
will merit eternal damnation for herself and
for every person that makes familiar with
her. And I say to that woman," says he,
" that she is a cursed woman, and I say to
you, let you not have intercourse or neigh-
bourliness with that woman but as much as
you'd have with a *dearg-daol*. Rise up now,
Dearg-Daol," says he, " and avoid the company of decent people henceforth."

The poor woman got up, and went out
the chapel door. There was no name on
her from that out but the *Dearg-Daol*. Her
own name and surname were put out of mind.
'Twas said that she had the evil eye. If
she'd look on a calf or a sheep that wasn't
her own, the animal would die. The women
were afraid to let their children out on the

street if the *Dearg-Daol* was going the road.

I married a comely girl when I was of the age of one-and-twenty. We had a little slip of a girl, and we had hopes of another child. One day when I was cutting turf in the bog, my wife was feeding the fowl on the street, when she saw—God between us and harm—the *Dearg-Daol* making on her up the bohereen, and she with the little, soft *pataire* of a child in her arms. An arm of the child was about the woman's neck, and her shawl covering her. Speech left my wife.

The *Dearg-Daol* laid the little girl in her mother's breast. My woman took notice that her clothes were wet.

" What happened the child ? " says she.

" Falling into Lochán na Luachra (the Pool of the Rushes), she did it," says the *Dearg-Daol*. " Looking for water-lilies she was. I was crossing the road, and I heard her scream. In over the dyke with me. It was only by dint of trouble I caught her."

" May God reward you," says my wife. The other woman went off before she had time to say more. My wife fetched the little wee thing inside, she dried her, and put her to sleep. When I came in from the bog she told me the story. The two of us prayed our blessing on the *Dearg-Daol* that night.

The day after, the little girl began prattling about the woman that saved her. "The water was in my mouth, and in my eyes, and in my ears," says she. "I saw shining sparks, and I heard a great noise ; I was slipping and slipping," says she ; "and then," says she, "I felt a hand about me, and she lifted me up and she kissed me. I thought it was at home, I was, when I was in her arms and her shawl about me," says she.

A couple of days after that my wife noticed the little thing away from her. We sought her for the length of two hours. When she came home she told us that she was after paying a visit to the woman that saved her. "She made a cake for me," says she. "She has ne'er a one in the house at all but herself, and she said to me I should go visiting her every evening."

Neither I nor my wife was able to say a

143

word against her. The *Dearg-Daol* was
after saving our girl's life, and it wouldn't
be natural to hinder the child going into her
house. From that day out the little girl
would go up the hill to her every day.

The neighbours said to us that it wasn't
right. There was a sort of suspicion on
ourselves that it wasn't right, but how
could we help it?

Would you believe me, people? From
the day the *Dearg-Daol* laid eyes on the
little girl, she began dwindling and dwindling, like a fire that wouldn't be mended.
She lost her appetite and her activity. After
a quarter she was only a shadow. After
another month she was in the churchyard.

The *Dearg-Daol* came down the mountain the day she was buried. She wouldn't
be let into the graveyard. She went her
road up the mountain again alone. My
heart bled for the creature, for I knew that
our trouble was no heavier than her trouble.
I myself went up the hill the morning of
the next day. I meant to say to her that
neither my wife nor myself had any up-
braiding for her. I knocked at the door.
I didn't get any answer. I went into the

THE ROADS

Rossnageeragh will mind till death the night the Dublin Man gave us the feast in the schoolhouse of Turlagh Beg. We had no name or surname for that same man ever but the "Dublin Man." Peatin Pharaig would say to us that he was a man who wrote for the newspapers. Peatin would read the Gaelic paper the mistress got every week, and it's a small thing he hadn't knowledge of, for there was discourse in that paper on the doings of the Western World and on the goings-on of the Eastern World, and there would be no bounds to the information Peatin would have to give us every Sunday at the chapel gate. He would say to us that the Dublin Man had a stack of money, for two hundred pounds in the year were coming to him out of the heart of that paper he wrote for every week.

The Dublin Man would pay a fortnight's or a month's visit to Turlagh every year. This very year he sent out word calling

149

poor and naked to a feast he was gathering
for us in the schoolhouse. He announced
that there would be music and dancing and
Gaelic speeches in it ; that there would be
a piper there from Carrowroe ; that Brigid
ni Mhainin would be there to give *Conntae
Mhuigheó* ; that Martin the Fisherman
would tell a Fenian story ; that old Una ni
Greelis would recite a poem if the creature
wouldn't have the asthma ; and that Marcuseen Mhichil Ruaidh would do a bout
of dancing unless the rheumatic pains would
be too bad on him. Nobody ever knew
Marcuseen to have the rheumatics but when
he'd be asked to dance. " Bedam, but I'm
dead with the pains for a week," he'd
always say when a dance would be hinted.
But no sooner would the piper start on
" Tatter Jack Walsh," than Marcuseen
would throw his old hat in the air, " hup !"
he'd say, and take the floor.

The family of Col Labhras were drinking tea the evening of the feast.

" Will we go to the schoolhouse to-night,
daddy ?" says Cuimin Col to his father.

" We will. Father Ronan said he'd like
all the people to go."

"Won't we have the spree!" says Cuimin.

"You'll stay at home, Nora," says the mother, "to mind the child."

Nora put a lip on herself, but she didn't speak.

After tea Col and his wife went into the room to ready themselves for the road.

"My sorrow that it's not a boy God made me," says Nora to her brother.

"*Muise*, why?" says Cuimin.

"For one reason better than another," says Nora. With that she gave a little slap to the child that was half-asleep and half-awake in the cradle. The child let a howl out of him.

"*Ara*, listen to the child," says Cuimin. "If my mother hears him crying, she'll take the ear off you."

"I don't care if she takes the two ears off me," says Nora.

"What's up with you?" Cuimin was washing himself, and he stopped to look over his shoulder at his sister, and the water streaming from his face.

"Tired of being made a little ass of by my mother and by everybody, I am," says

Nora. "I working from morning till night, and ye at your ease. Ye going to the spree to-night, and I sitting here nursing this child. 'You'll stay at home, Nora, to mind the child,' says my mother. That's always the way. It's a pity it's not a boy God made me."

Cuimin was drying his face meanwhile, and " s-s-s-s-s " coming out of him like a person would be grooming a horse.

"It's a pity, right enough," says he, when he was able to speak.

He threw the towel from him, he put his head to one side, and looked complacently at himself in the glass was hanging on the wall.

"A parting in my hair now," says he, " and I'll be first-class."

"Are you ready, Cuimin?" says his father, coming out of the room.

"I am."

"We'll be stirring on then."

The mother came out.

"If he there is crying, Nora," says she, "give him a drink of milk out of the bottle."

Nora didn't say a word. She remained sitting on the stool beside the cradle, and her

chin laid in her two hands and her two
elbows stuck on her knees.   She heard her
father and her mother and Cuimin going out
the door and across the street ; she knew by
their voices that they were going down the
bohereen.   The voices died away, and she understood that they were after taking the road.

Nora began making fancy pictures in her
mind.   She saw, she thought, the fine, level
road and it white under the moonlight.   The
people were in groups making for the schoolhouse.   The Rossnageeragh folk were coming out the road, and the Garumna folk
journeying round by the mistress's house,
and the Kilbrickan folk crowding down the
hill, and the Turlagh Beg's crowding likewise ; there was a band from Turlagh, and
an odd sprinkling from Glencaha, and one
or two out of Inver coming in the road.
She imagined her own people were at the
school gate by now.   They were going up
the path.   They were entering in the door.
The schoolhouse was well-nigh full, and
still no end to the coming of the people.
There were lamps hung on the walls, and
the house as bright as it would be in the
middle of day.   Father Ronan was there,

and he going from person to person and
bidding welcome to everybody. The Dublin
Man was there, and he as nice and friendly-
like as ever. The mistress was there, and
the master and mistress from Gortmore, and
the lace-instructress. The schoolgirls sitting
together on the front benches. Weren't
they to sing a song? She saw, she thought,
Maire Sean Mor, and Maire Pheatin Johnny,
and Babeen Col Marcus, and the Boatman's
Brigid, and her red head on her, and Brigid
Caitin ni Fhiannachta, with her mouth open
as usual. The girls were looking round and
nudging one another, and asking one another
where was Nora Col Labhras. The schoolhouse was packed to the door now. Father
Ronan was striking his two hands together.
They were stopping from talk and from
whispering. Father Ronan was speaking to
them. He was speaking comically. Everybody was laughing. He was calling on the
schoolgirls to give their song. They were
getting up and going to the head of the
room and bowing to the people.

" My sorrow, that I'm not there," says
poor Nora to herself, and she laid her face
in her palms and began crying.

THE ROADS

She stopped crying, suddenly. She hung
her head, and rubbed a palm to her eyes.

It wasn't right, says she in her own mind.
It wasn't right, just, or decent. Why should
she be kept at home? Why should they
always keep her at home? If she was
a boy she'd be let out. Since she was only
a girl they would keep her at home. She
was, as she had said to Cuimin that evening,
only a little ass of a girl. She wouldn't put
up with it any longer. She would have her
own way. She would be as free as any boy
that came or went. It's often before that
she set her mind to the deed. She would
do the deed that night.

It's often Nora thought that it would be a
fine life to be going like a flying hawk,
independent of everybody. The roads of
Ireland before her, and her face on them;
the back of her head to home and hardship
and the vexation of her people. She going
from village to village, and from glen to
glen. The fine, level road before her, fields
on both sides of her, little, well-sheltered
houses on the slopes of the hills. If she'd
get tired she could stretch back by the side
of a ditch, or she could go into some house

and ask the good woman for a drink of milk
and a seat by the fire. To make the night's
sleep in some wood under the shadow of
trees, and to rise early in the morning and
stretch out again under the lovely fresh air.
If she wanted food (and it's likely she would
want it), she would do a day's work here
and a day's work there, and she would be
full-satisfied if she got a cup of tea and a
crumb of bread in payment for it. Wouldn't
it be a fine life that, besides being a little ass
of a girl at home, feeding the hens and
minding the child!

It's not as a girl she'd go, but as a boy.
No one in life would know that it's not a
boy was in it. When she'd cut her hair
and put on herself a suit of Cuimin's
bawneens, who would know that it's a girl
she was?

It's often Nora took that counsel to herself, but the fear would never let her put it
in practice. She never had right leave for
it. Her mother would always be in the
house, and no sooner would she be gone
than she'd feel wanted. But she had leave
now. None of them would be back in the
house for another hour of the clock, at the

least. She'd have a power of time to change
her clothes, and to go off unbeknown to the
world. She would meet nobody on the road,
for all the people were gathered in the
schoolhouse. She would have time to go
as far as Ellery to-night and to sleep in the
wood. She would rise early on the morrow
morning, and she would take the road before
anybody would be astir.

She jumped from the stool. There were
scissors in the drawer of the dresser. It
wasn't long till she had a hold of them, and
snip! snap! She cut off her back hair,
and the fringe that was on her brow, and
each ringleted tress that was on her, in one
attack. She looked at herself in the glass.
A inghean O! isn't it bald and bare she looked.
She gathered the curls of hair from the
floor, and she hid them in an old box. Over
with her then to the place where a clean
suit of bawneens belonging to Cuimin was
hanging on a nail. Down with her on her
knees searching for a shirt of Cuimin's that
was in a lower drawer of the dresser. She
threw the clothes on the floor beside the fire.

Here she is now taking off her own share
of clothes in a hurry. She threw her

157

dress and her little blouse and her shift into
a chest that was under the table. She put
Cuimin's shirt on herself. She stuck her
legs into the breeches, and she pulled them
up on herself. She minded then that she
had neither belt nor gallowses. She'd have
to make a belt out of an old piece of cord.
She put the jacket on herself. She looked
in the glass, and she started. It's how she
thought Cuimin was before her! She
looked over her shoulder, but she didn't
see anybody. It's then she minded that it's
her own self was looking at her, and she
laughed. But if she did itself, she was a
little scared. If she'd a cap now she'd be
ready for the road. Yes, she knew where
there was an old cap of Cuimin's. She got
it, and put it on her head. Farewell for
ever now to the old life, and a hundred
welcomes to the new!

When she was at the door she turned
back and she crept over to the cradle. The
child was sound asleep. She bent down
and she gave a kiss to the baby, a little,
little, light kiss in on his forehead. She
stole on the tips of her toes to the door,
opened it gently, went out on the street,

and shut the door quietly after her. Across
the street with her, and down the bohereen.
It was short till she took the road to herself. She pressed on then towards Turlagh
Beg.

It was short till she saw the schoolhouse
by the side of the road. There was a fine
light burning through the windows. She
heard a noise, as if they'd be laughing and
clapping hands within. Over across the
fence with her, and up the school path.
She went round to the back of the house.
The windows were high enough, but she
raised herself up till she'd a view of what
was going on inside. Father Ronan was
speaking. He stopped, and O, Lord ! —
the people began getting up. It was plain
that the fun was over, and that they were
about to separate to go home. What
would she do, if she'd be seen?

She threw a leap from the window. Her
foot slipped from her, coming down on the
ground, and she got a drop. She very
nearly screamed out, but she minded herself
in time. Her knee was a little hurt, she
thought. The people were out on the
school yard by that. She must stay in

hiding till they were all gone. She moved into the wall as close as she could. She heard the people talking and laughing, and she knew that they were scattering after one another.

What was that? The voices of people coming towards her; the sound of a foot-step on the path beside her! It's then she minded that there was a short-cut across the back of the house, and that there might be some people going the short-cut. Likely, her own people would be going that way, for it was a little shorter than round by the high road. A little knot came towards her; she recognized by their voices that they were Peatin Johnny's people. They passed. Another little knot; the Boatman's family. They drew that close to her that Eamonn trod on her poor, bare, little foot. She almost let a cry out of her the second time, but she didn't—she only squeezed herself tighter to the wall. Another crowd was coming: O, Great God, her own people! Cuimin was saying, " Wasn't it wonderful, Marcuseen's dancing!" Her mother's dress brushed Nora's cheek going by: she didn't draw her breath all that

time. A company or two more went
past. She listened for a spell. Nobody
else was coming. It's how they were all
gone, said she to herself. Out with her
from her hiding-place, and she tore across
the path. Plimp! She ran against somebody. Two big hands were about her.
She heard a man's voice. She recognized
the voice. The priest that was in it.

"Who have I?" says Father Ronan.

She told a lie. What else had she to
say?

"Cuimin Col Labhras, Father," says she.

He laid a hand on each shoulder of her,
and looked down on her. She had her
head bent.

"I thought you went home with your
father and mother," says he.

"I did, Father, but I lost my cap and I
came back looking for it."

"Isn't your cap on your head?"

"I found it on the path."

"Aren't your father and mother gone
the short-cut?"

"They are, Father, but I am going the
road so that I'll be with the other boys."

"Off with you, then, or the ghosts'll

catch you!" With that Father Ronan
let her go from him.

"May God give you good-night, Father,"
says she. She didn't mind to take off her
cap, but it's how she curtseyed to the
priest after the manner of girls! If the
priest took notice of that much he hadn't
time to say a word, for she was gone in the
turning of your hand.

Her two cheeks were red-hot with shame,
and she giving face on the road. She was
after telling four big lies to the priest!
She was afraid that those lies were a
terrible sin on her soul. She was afraid
going that lonesome road in the darkness of the night, and that burthen on
her heart. The night was very black.
There was a little brightening on her right
hand. The lake of Turlagh Beg that was
in it. There rose some bird, a curlew or a
snipe, from the brink of the lake, letting
mournful cries out of it. Nora started
when she heard the bird's voice, that
suddenly, and the drumming of its wings.
She hurried on, and her heart beating against
her breast. She left Turlagh Beg behind
her, and faced the long, straight road that

162

leads to the Crosses of Kilbrickan. It's
with trouble she recognized the shape of the
houses on the hill when she reached the
Crosses. There was a light in the house of
Peadar O Neachtain, and she heard voices
from the side of Snamh-Bo. She followed
on, drawing on Turlagh. When she reached
the Bog Hill the moon came out, and she
saw from her the scar of the hills. There
came a great cloud across the face of the
moon, and it seemed to her that it's double
dark the night was then. Terror seized her,
for she minded that Cnoc-a'-Leachta (the
Hill of the Grave) wasn't far off, and that
the graveyard would be on her right hand
then. It's often she heard that was an
evil place in the middle of the night. She
sharpened her pace ; she began running.
She thought that she was being followed ;
that there was a bare-footed woman tread-
ing almost on her heels ; that there was a
thin, black man travelling alongside her ;
that there was a child, and a white shirt on
him, going the road before her. She opened
her mouth to let a screech out of her, but
there didn't come a sound from her. She
was in a cold sweat. Her legs were bending

under her. She nearly fell in a heap on
the road. She was at Cnoc-a'-Leachta
about that time. It seemed to her that
Cill Eoin was full of ghosts. She minded
the word the priest said " Have a care, or
the ghosts'll catch you." They were on
her ! She heard, she thought, the " plub-
plab " of naked feet on the road. She
turned to her left hand and she gave a leap
over the ditch. She went near to being
drowned in a deal-hole that was between
her and the wood, unbeknown to her. She
twisted her foot trying to save herself, and
she felt pain. On with her, reeling. She
was in the fields of Ellery then. She saw
the lamp of the lake through the branches.
A tree-root took a stumble out of her, and
she fell. She lost her senses.

.   .   .   .

After a very long time she imagined that
the place was filled with a sort of half-light,
a light that was between the light of the
sun and the light of the moon. She saw,
very clearly, the feet of the trees, and them
dark against a yellowish-green sky. She
never saw a sky of that colour before, and it
was beautiful to her. She heard a footstep,

164

and she understood that there was someone
coming towards her up from the lake. She
knew in some manner that a prodigious
miracle was about to be shown her, and that
someone was to suffer there some awful
passion. She hadn't long to wait till she
saw a young man struggling wearily through
the tangle of the wood. He had his head
bent, and the appearance of great sorrow on
him. Nora recognised him. The Son of
Mary that was in it, and she knew that He
was journeying all alone to His death.

The Man threw himself on His knees, and
He began praying. Nora didn't hear one
word from Him, but she understood in her
heart what He was saying. He was asking
His Eternal Father to send someone to Him
who would side with Him against His
enemies, and who would bear half of His
burthen. Nora wished to rise and to go to
Him, but she couldn't stir out of the place
she was in.

She heard a noise, and the place was filled
with armed men. She saw dark, devilish
faces and grey swords and edged weapons.
The gentle Man was seized outrageously,
and His share of clothes torn from Him, and

165

He was scourged with scourges there till His
body was in a bloody mass and in an ever-
lasting wound from His head to the soles of
His feet. A thorny crown was put then on
His gentle head, and a cross was laid on His
shoulders, and He went before Him, heavy-
footed, pitifully, the sorrowful way of His
journey to Calvary. The chain that was
tying Nora's tongue and limbs till that broke,
and she cried aloud:

"Let me go with You, Jesus, and carry
Your cross for You!"

.   .   .   .   .   .

She felt a hand on her shoulder. She
looked up. She saw her father's face.

"What's on my little girl, or why did
she go from us?" says her father's voice.

He lifted her in his arms and he brought her
home. She lay on her bed till the end of a
month after that. She was out of her mind
for half of that time, and she thought at times
that she was going the road, like a lone,
wild-goose, and asking knowledge of the
way of people; and she thought at other
times that she was lying in under a tree in
Ellery, and that she was watching again the
passion of that gentle Man, and she trying

to help Him, but without power to help
him. That wandering went out of her
mind at long last, and she understood she
was at home again. And when she recognised her mother's face her heart was filled
with consolation, and she asked her to put
the child into the bed with her, and when
he was put into the bed she kissed him
lovingly.

" Oh, mameen," says she, " I thought I
wouldn't see you or my father or Cuimin or
the child ever again. Were ye here all
that time ? "

" We were, white lamb," says her mother.

" I'll stay in the place where ye are," says
she. " Oh, mameen, heart, the roads were
very dark. . . . And I'll never strike
the child again,"—and she gave him another
little kiss.

The child put his arm about her neck,
and he curled himself up in the bed at his
full ease.

BRIGID OF THE SONGS

Brigid of the Songs was the most famous singer in Rossnageeragh, not only in my time but in my father's time. It's said that she could wile the song-thrush from the branch with the sweetness of the music that God gave her; and I would believe it, for it's often she wiled me and other lads besides from our dinner or our supper. I'd be a rich man to-day if I had a shilling for every time I stopped outside her door, on my way home from school, listening to her share of songs; and my father told me that it's often and often he did the same thing when he was a lad going to school. It was a tradition among the people that it was from Raftery himself that Brigid learned "*Conntae Mhuigheó*" (The County of Mayo), and isn't it with the "*Conntae Mhuigheó*" that she drew the big tears out of the eyes of John MacHale one time he was on a visit here, along with our own Bishop, a year exactly before I was born?

A thing that's no wonder, when we heard

171

that there was to be a Feis in Moykeeran, we all settled in our minds that it's Brigid would have the prize for the singing, if she'd enter for it. There was no other person, neither men-singers nor women-singers, half as good as she was in the seven parishes. She couldn't be beaten, if right was to be done. She would put wonderment on the people of Moykeeran and on the grand folk would be in it out of Galway and out of Tuam. She would earn name and fame for Rossnageeragh. She would win the prize easy, and she would be sent to Dublin to sing a song at the Oireachtas. There was a sort of hesitation on Brigid at first. She was too old, she said. Her voice wasn't as good as it used be. She hadn't her wind. A share of her songs were going out of her memory. She didn't want a prize. Didn't the men of Ireland know that she was the best singer in Iar-Connacht? Didn't Raftery praise her, didn't Colm Wallace make a song in her honour, didn't she draw tears out of the eyes of John MacHale? Brigid said that much and seven times more; but it was plain, at the same time, that there was a wish on her to go to the Feis, and we all knew that she would go. To make a short story of it, we were at her until we took a promise out of her that she would go.

She went. It's well I remember the day of the Feis. The world of Ireland was there, you'd think. The house was overflowing with poor people and with rich people, with noble folk and with lowly folk, with strong, active youths, and with withered, done old people. There were priests and friars there from every art. There were doctors and lawyers there from Tuam and from Galway and from Uachtar Ard. There were newspaper people there from Dublin. There was a lord's son there from England. The full of people went up, singing songs. Brigid went up. We were at the back of the house, listening to her. She began. There was a little bashfulness on her at the start, and her voice was too low. But she came to herself in time, according as she was stirring out into the song, and she took tears out of the eyes of the gathering with the last verse. There was great cheering when she had finished, and she coming down. *We* put a shout out of us you'd think would crack the roof of the house. A young girl went up. Her voice was a long way better than Brigid's, but, we thought, there was not the same sadness nor sweetness in the song as there was in Brigid's. She came down. The people cheered again, but I didn't notice that anybody was crying. One of the judges got up. He praised Brigid greatly. He praised the young girl greatly, too. He was very tedious.

"Who won the prize?" says one of us at last, when our share of patience was exhausted.

"Oh, the prize!" says he. "Well, in regard to the prize, we are giving it to Nora Cassidy (the young girl), but we are considering the award of a special prize to Brígid ní Mhainín (our Brigid). Nora Cassidy will be sent to Dublin to sing a song at the Oireachtas."

The Moykeeran people applauded, for it was out of Moykeeran that Nora Cassidy was. We didn't say anything. We looked over at Brigid. Her face was grey-white, and she trembling in every limb.

"What did you say, sir, please?" says

174

she in a strange voice. "Is it I that have the prize?"

"We are considering the award of a special prize to you, my good woman, as you shaped so excellently—you did that,—but it's to Nora Cassidy that the Feis prize is given."

Brigid didn't speak a word; but it's how she rose up, and without looking either to the right hand or to the left, she went out the door. She took the road to Rossnageeragh, and she was before us when we reached the village late in the night.

.   .   .   .   .   .

The Oireachtas was to be in Dublin the week after. We were a sad crowd, remembering that Brigid of the Songs wouldn't be there. We were full sure that fair play wasn't done her in Moykeeran, and we thought that if she'd go to Dublin she'd get satisfaction. But alas! we had no money to send her there, and if we had itself we knew that she wouldn't take it from us. We were arguing the question one evening at the gable of the Boatman's house, when who should come up but little Martin Connolly, at a full run, and he said to us

that Brigid of the Songs was gone, the lock
on the door, and no tale or tidings to be got
of her.

We didn't know what happened her
until a fortnight's time after that. Here's
how it fell out. When she heard that the
Oireachtas was to be in Dublin on such a
day, she said to herself that she would be
there if she lived. She didn't let on to
anyone, but went off with herself in the
night-time, walking. She had only a florin
piece in her pocket. She didn't know
where Dublin was, nor how far it was
away. She followed her nose, it's like,
asking the road of the people she met,
tramping always, until she'd left behind her
Cashlagh, and Spiddal, and Galway, and
Oranmore, and Athenry, and Kilconnell,
and Ballinasloe, and Athlone, and Mullingar,
and Maynooth, until at last she saw from
her the houses of Dublin. It's like that her
share of money was spent long before that,
and nobody will ever know how the creature
lived on that long, lonesome journey. But
one evening when the Oireachtas was in full
swing in the big hall in Dublin, a country-
woman was seen coming in the door, her

feet cut and bleeding with the hard stones of the road, her share of clothes speckled with dust and dirt, and she weary, worn-out and exhausted.

She sat down. People were singing in the old style. Brígid ní Mhainín from Rossnageeragh was called on (for we had entered her name in hopes that we'd be able to send her). The old woman rose, went up, and started "*Conntae Mhuigheó.*"

When she finished the house was in one ree-raw with shouts, it was that fine. She was told to sing another song. She began on the "*Sail Og Ruadh*" (The Red Willow). She had only the first line of the second verse said when there came some wandering in her head. She stopped and she began again. The wandering came on her a second time, then a trembling, and she fell in a faint on the stage. She was carried out of the hall. A doctor came to examine her.

"She is dying from the hunger and the hardship," says he.

While that was going on, great shouts were heard inside the hall. One of the judges came out in a hurry.

THE THIEF

One day when the boys of Gortmore were
let out from school, after the Glencaha boys
and the Derrybanniv boys had gone east, the
Turlagh boys and the Inver boys stayed to
have a while's chat before separating at the
Rossnageeragh road. The master's house
is exactly at the head of the road, its back
to the hill and its face to Loch Ellery.

"I heard that the master's bees were
swarming," says Michileen Bartly Enda.

"In with you into the garden till we
look at them," says Daragh Barbara of the
Bridge.

"I'm afraid," says Michileen.

"What are you afraid of?" says Daragh.

"By my word, the master and the mistress
will be out presently."

"Who'll stay to give us word when the
master will be coming?" says Daragh.

"I will," says little Anthony Manning.

"That'll do," says Daragh. "Let a
whistle when you see him leaving the school."

In over the fence with him. In over the
fence with the other boys after him.

" Have a care that none of you will get
a sting," says Anthony.

" Little fear," says Daragh. And off
forever with them.

Anthony sat on the fence, and his back to
the road. He could see the master over his
right shoulder if he'd leave the schoolhouse.
What a nice garden the master had, thought
Anthony. He had rose-trees and gooseberry-
trees and apple-trees. He had little white
stones round the path. He had big white
stones in a pretty rockery, and moss and
maiden-hair fern and common fern growing
between them. He had . . .

Anthony saw a wonder greater than any
wonder the master had in the garden. He
saw a little, beautiful wee house under the
shade of one of the rose-trees; it made of
wood; two storys in it; white colour on
the lower story and red colour on the upper
story; a little green door on it; three
windows of glass on it, one downstairs and
two upstairs; house furniture in it, between
tables and chairs and beds and delf, and the
rest; and, says Anthony to himself, look at
the lady of the house sitting in the door!

Anthony never saw a doll's house before,

and it was a wonder to him, its neatness and order, for a toy. He knew that it belonged to the master's little girl, little Nance. A pity that his own little sister hadn't one like it— Eibhlin, the creature, that was stretched on her bed for a long three months, and she weak and sick! A pity she hadn't the doll itself! Anthony put the covetousness of his heart in that doll for Eibhlin. He looked over his right shoulder—neither master nor mistress was to be seen. He looked over his left shoulder—the other boys were out of sight. He didn't think the second thought. He gave his best leap from the fence; he seized the doll; he stuck it under his jacket; he clambered out over the ditch again, and away with him home.

"I have a present for you," says he to Eibhlin, when he reached the house. "Look!" and with that he showed her the doll.

There came a blush on the wasted cheeks of the little sick girl, and a light into her eyes.

"*Ora*, Anthony, love, where did you get it?" says she.

"The master's little Nance, that sent it to you for a present," says Anthony.

Their mother came in.

"Oh, mameen, treasure," says Eibhlin, "look at the present that the master's little Nance sent me!"

"In earnest?" says the mother.

"Surely," says Eibhlin. "Anthony, it was, that brought it in to me now."

Anthony looked down at his feet, and began counting the toes that were on them.

"My own pet," says the mother, "isn't it she that was good to you! *Muise*, Nance! I'll go bail that that present will put great improvement on my little girl."

And there came tears in the mother's eyes out of gratitude to little Nance because she remembered the sick child. Though he wasn't able to look his mother between the eyes, or at Eibhlin, with the dint of fear, Anthony was glad that he committed the theft.

He was afraid to say his prayers that night, and he lay down on his bed without as much as an "Our Father." He couldn't say the Act of Contrition, for it wasn't truthfully he'd be able to say to God that he was sorry for that sin. It's often he started in the night, imagining that little

Nance was coming seeking the doll from
Eibhlin, that the master was taxing him
with the robbery before the school, that
there was a miraculous swarm of bees rising
against him, and Daragh Barbara of the
Bridge and the other boys exciting them
with shouts and with the music of drums.
But the next morning he said to himself:
"I don't care. The doll will make Eibhlin
better."

When he went to school the boys asked
him why he went off unawares the evening
before that, and he after promising them
he'd keep watch.

"My mother sent for me," says Anthony.
"She'd a task for me."

When little Nance came into the school,
Anthony looked at her under his brows.
He fancied that she was after being crying;
he thought that he saw the track of the
tears on her cheeks. The first time the
master called him by his name he jumped,
because he thought that he was going to tax
him with the fault or to cross-question him
about the doll. He never put in as miserable
a day as that day at school. But when he
went home and saw the great improvement

on Eibhlin, and she sitting up in the bed for the first time for a month, and the doll clasped in her arms, says he to himself: " I don't care. The doll is making Eibhlin better."

In his bed in the night-time he had bad dreams again. He thought that the master was after telling the police that he stole the doll, and that they were on his track ; he imagined one time that there was a police-man hiding under the bed and that there was another hunkering behind the window-curtain. He screamed out in his sleep.

" What's on you? " says his father to him.

" The peeler that's going to take me," says Anthony.

" You're only rambling, boy," says his father to him. " There's no peeler in it. Go to sleep."

There was the misery of the world on the poor fellow from that out. He used think they would be pointing fingers at him, and he going the road. He used think they would be shaking their heads and saying to each other, " There's a thief," or, " Did you hear what Anthony Pharaig Manning did? Her doll he stole from the master's little Nance. Now what do you say?" But he didn't suffer rightly till he went to Mass on Sunday and till Father Ronan started preaching a sermon on the Seventh Commandment: "Thou shalt not steal; and if you commit a theft it will not be forgiven you until you make restitution." Anthony was full sure that it was a mortal sin. He knew that he ought to go to confession and tell the sin to the priest. But he couldn't go to confession, for he knew that the priest would say to him that he must give the doll back. And he wouldn't give the doll back. He hardened his heart and he said that he'd never give the doll back, for that the doll was making Eibhlin better every day.

One evening he was sitting by the bed-foot in serious talk with Eibhlin when his mother ran in in a hurry, and says she —

"Here's the mistress and little Nance coming up the bohereen!"

Anthony wished the earth would open and swallow him. His face was red up to his two ears. He was in a sweat. He wasn't able to say a word or to think a thought. But these words were running through his head : " They'll take the doll from Eibhlin." It was all the same to him what they'd say or what they'd do to himself. The only answer he'd have would be, " The doll's making Eibhlin better."

The mistress and little Nance came into the room. Anthony got up. He couldn't look them in the face. He began at his old clatter, counting the toes of his feet. Five on each foot ; four toes and a big toe ; or three toes, a big toe, and a little toe ; that's five ; twice five are ten ; ten in all. He couldn't add to their number or take from them. His mother was talking, the mistress was talking, but Anthony paid no heed to them. He was waiting till something would be said about the doll. There was nothing for him to do till that but count his toes. One, two, three . . .

What was that? Eibhlin was referring to the doll. Anthony listened now.

" Wasn't it good of you to send me the doll?" she was saying to Nance. " From the day Anthony brought it in to me a change began coming on me."

" It did that," says her mother. " We'll be forever grateful to you for that same doll

you sent to her. May God increase your
store, and may He requite you for it a
thousand times."

Neither Nance nor the mistress spoke.
Anthony looked at Nance shyly. His two
eyes were stuck in the doll, for the doll was
lying cosy in the bed beside Eibhlin. It
had its mouth half open, and the wonder of
the world on it at the sayings of Eibhlin
and her mother.

"It's with trouble I believed Anthony
when he brought it into me," says Eibhlin,
"and when he told me you sent it to me as
a present."

Nance looked over at Anthony. Anthony
lifted his head slowly, and their eyes met.
It will never be known what Nance read in
Anthony's eyes. What Anthony read in
Nance's eyes was mercy, love and sweetness.
Nance spoke to Eibhlin.

"Do you like it?" says she.

"Over anything," says Eibhlin. I'd
rather it than anything I have in the
world."

"I have the little house it lives in," says
Nance. "I must send it to you. Anthony
will bring it to you to-morrow."

"*Ora!*" says Eibhlin, and she clapping her two little thin palms together.

"You'll miss it, love," says Eibhlin's mother to Nance.

"No," said Nance. "It will put more improvement on Eibhlin. I have lots of things."

"Let her do it, Cait," said the mistress to the mother.

"Ye are too good," says the poor woman.

Anthony thought that it's dreaming he was. Or he thought that it's not a person of this world little Nance was at all, but an angel come down out of heaven. He wanted to go on his knees to her.

When the mistress and little Nance went off, Anthony ran out the back door and tore across the garden, so that he'd be before them at the bohereen-foot, and they going out on the road.

"Nance," says he, "I s-stole it,—the d-doll."

"Never mind, Anthony," says Nance, "you did good to Eibhlin."

Anthony stood like a stake in the road, and he couldn't speak another word.

Isn't it he was proud bringing the doll's

house home to Eibhlin after school the next day! And isn't it they had the fun that evening settling the house and polishing the furniture and putting the doll to sleep on its little bed!

The Saturday following Anthony went to confession, and told his sin to the priest. The penance the priest put on him was to clean the doll's house once in the week for Eibhlin, till she would be strong enough to clean it herself. Eibhlin was strong enough for it by the end of a month. By the end of another month she was at school again.

There wasn't a Saturday evening from that out that they wouldn't hear a little, light tapping at the master's door. On the mistress going out Anthony would be standing at the door.

"Here's a little present for Nance," he'd say, stretching towards her half-a-dozen duck's eggs, or a bunch of heather, or, at the least, the full of his fist of *duileasg*, and then he'd brush off with him without giving the mistress time to say "thank you."

191

THE KEENING WOMAN

I

"Coilin," says my father to me one morning after the breakfast, and I putting my books together to be stirring to school— "Coilin," says he, "I have a task for you to-day. Sean will tell the master it was myself kept you at home to-day, or it's the way he'll be thinking you're miching, like you were last week. Let you not forget now, Sean."

"I will not, father," says Sean, and a lip on him. He wasn't too thankful it to be said that it's not for him my father had the task. This son was well satisfied, for my lessons were always a trouble to me, and the master promised me a beating the day before unless I'd have them at the tip of my mouth the next day.

"What you'll do, Coilin," says my father when Sean was gone off, "is to bring the ass and the little car with you to Screeb, and draw home a load of sedge. Michileen

Maire is cutting it for me. We'll be starting, with God's help, to put the new roof on the house after to-morrow, if the weather stands."

"Michileen took the ass and car with him this morning," says I.

"You'll have to leg it, then, *a mhic O*," says my father. "As soon as Michileen has an ass-load cut, fetch it home with you on the car, and let Michileen tear till he's black. We might draw the other share to-morrow."

It wasn't long till I was knocking steps out of the road. I gave my back to Kilbrickan and my face to Turlagh. I left Turlagh behind me, and I made for Gortmore. I stood a spell looking at an oared boat that was on Loch Ellery, and another spell playing with some Inver boys that were late going to Gortmore school. I left them at the school gate, and I reached Glencaha. I stood, for the third time, watching a big eagle that was sunning himself on Carrigacapple. East with me, then, till I was in Derrybanniv, and the hour and a half wasn't spent when I cleared Glashaduff bridge.

196

THE KEENING WOMAN

There was a house that time a couple of
hundred yards east from the bridge, near
the road, on your right-hand side and you
drawing towards Screeb. It was often before
that that I saw an old woman standing in
the door of that house, but I had no
acquaintance on her, nor did she ever put
talk or topic on me. A tall, thin woman
she was, her head as white as the snow,
and two dark eyes, as they would be two
burning sods, flaming in her head. She
was a woman that would scare me if I met
her in a lonely place in the night. Times
she would be knitting or carding, and she
crooning low to herself; but the thing she
would be mostly doing when I travelled,
would be standing in the door, and looking
from her up and down the road, exactly as
she'd be waiting for someone that would be
away from her, and she expecting him home.

She was standing there that morning as
usual, her hand to her eyes, and she staring
up the road. When she saw me going
past, she nodded her head to me. I went
over to her.

"Do you see a person at all coming up
the road?" says she.

" I don't," says I.

" I thought I saw someone. It can't be that I'm astray. See, isn't that a young man making up on us?" says she.

" Devil a one do I see," says I. "There's not a person at all between the spot we're on and the turning of the road."

" I was astray, then," says she. " My sight isn't as good as it was. I thought I saw him coming. I don't know what's keeping him."

" Who's away from you?" says myself.

" My son that's away from me," says she.

" Is he long away?"

" This morning he went to Uachtar Ard."

" But, sure, he couldn't be here for a while," says I. " You'd think he'd barely be in Uachtar Ard by now, and he doing his best, unless it was by the morning train he went from the Burnt House."

" What's this I'm saying?" says she. " It's not to-day he went, but yesterday,—or the day ere yesterday, maybe. . . . I'm losing my wits."

" If it's on the train he's coming," says I, "he'll not be here for a couple of hours yet."

"On the train?" says she. "What train?"

"The train that does be at the Burnt House at noon."

"He didn't say a word about a train," says she. "There was no train coming as far as the Burnt House yesterday."

"Isn't there a train coming to the Burnt House these years?" says I, wondering greatly. She didn't give me any answer, however. She was staring up the road again. There came a sort of dread on me of her, and I was about gathering off.

"If you see him on the road," says she, "tell him to make hurry."

"I've no acquaintance on him," says I.

"You'd know him easy. He's the play-boy of the people. A young, active lad, and he well set-up. He has a white head on him, like is on yourself, and grey eyes . . . like his father had. Bawneens he's wearing."

"If I see him," says I, "I'll tell him you're waiting for him."

"Do, son," says she.

With that I stirred on with me east, and left her standing in the door.

   •   •   •   •   •   •

She was there still, and I coming home a
couple of hours after that, and the load of
sedge on the car.

"He didn't come yet?" says I to
her.

"No, *a mhuirnín*. You didn't see him?"

"No."

"No? What can have happened him?"

There were signs of rain on the day.

"Come in till the shower's over," says
she. "It's seldom I do have company."

I left the ass and the little car on the
road, and I went into the house.

"Sit and drink a cup of milk," says
she.

I sat on the bench in the corner, and she
gave me a drink of milk and a morsel of
bread. I was looking all round the house,
and I eating and drinking. There was a
chair beside the fire, and a white shirt and a
suit of clothes laid on it.

"I have these ready against he will
come," says she. "I washed the bawneens
yesterday after his departing,—no, the day
ere yesterday—I don't know right which
day I washed them; but, anyhow, they'll
be clean and dry before him when he does

come. . . . What's your own name?"
says she, suddenly, after a spell of silence.

I told her.

"*Muise*, my love you are!" says she.
"The very name that was—that is—on my
own son. Whose are you?"

I told her.

"And do you say you're a son of Sean
Feichin's?" says she. "Your father was in
the public-house in Uachtar Ard that night.
. . ." She stopped suddenly with that,
and there came some change on her. She
put her hand to her head. You'd think
that it's madness was struck on her. She
sat before the fire then, and she stayed for a
while dreaming into the heart of the fire.
It was short till she began moving herself
to and fro over the fire, and crooning or
keening in a low voice. I didn't understand
the words right, or it would be better for
me to say that it's not on the words I was
thinking but on the music. It seemed to me
that there was the loneliness of the hills in
the dead time of night, or the loneliness of
the grave when nothing stirs in it but
worms, in that music. Here are the words
as I heard them from my father after that :—

THE KEENING WOMAN

Sorrow on death, it is it that blackened my heart,
That carried off my love and that left me ruined,
Without friend, without companion under the
    roof of my house
But this sorrow in my middle, and I lamenting.

Going the mountain one evening,
The birds spoke to me sorrowfully,
The melodious snipe and the voiceful curlew,
Telling me that my treasure was dead.

I called on you, and your voice I did not hear,
I called again, and an answer I did not get.
I kissed your mouth, and O God, wasn't it cold!
Och, it's cold your bed is in the lonely graveyard.

And O sod-green grave, where my child is,
O narrow, little grave, since you are his bed,
My blessing on you, and the thousand blessings
On the green sods that are over my pet.

Sorrow on death, its blessing is not possible—
It lays fresh and withered together ;
And, O pleasant little son, it is it is my affliction,
Your sweet body to be making clay !

When she had that finished, she kept on
moving herself to and fro, and lamenting
in a low voice. It was a lonesome place
to be, in that backward house, and you to
have no company but yon solitary old

woman, mourning to herself by the fireside. There came a dread and a creeping
on me, and I rose to my feet.

"It's time for me to be going home,"
says I. "The evening's clearing."

"Come here," says she to me.

I went hither to her. She laid her two
hands softly on my head, and she kissed my
forehead.

"The protection of God to you, little
son," says she. "May He let the harm of
the year over you, and may He increase the
good fortune and happiness of the year to
you and to your family."

With that she freed me from her. I left
the house, and pushed on home with me.

.   .   .   .

"Where were you, Coilin, when the
shower caught you?" says my mother to me
that night. "It didn't do you any hurt."

"I waited in the house of yon old woman
on the east side of Glashaduff bridge," says
I. "She was talking to me about her son.
He's in Uachtar Ard these two days, and
she doesn't know why he hasn't come home
ere this."

My father looked over at my mother.

"The Keening Woman," says he.

" Who is she?" says I.

" The Keening Woman," says my father.
" Muirne of the Keens."

" Why was that name given to her?"
says I.

" For the keens she does be making,"
answered my father. "She's the most
famous keening-woman in Connemara or
in the Joyce Country. She's always sent
for when anyone dies. She keened my
father, and there's a chance but she'll keen
myself. But, may God comfort her, it's
her own dead she does be keening always,
it's all the same what corpse is in the
house."

" And what's her son doing in Uachtar
Ard?" says I.

" Her son died twenty years since,
Coilin," says my mother.

" He didn't die at all," says my father,
and a very black look on him. " *He was
murdered.*"

" Who murdered him?"

It's seldom I saw my father angry, but
it's awful his anger was when it would

rise up in him. He took a start out of me when he spoke again, he was that angry.

"Who murdered your own grandfather? Who drew the red blood out of my grandmother's shoulders with a lash? Who would do it but the English? My curse on —"

My mother rose, and she put her hand on his mouth.

"Don't give your curse to anyone, Sean," says she. My mother was that kind-hearted, she wouldn't like to throw the bad word at the devil himself. I believe she'd have pity in her heart for Cain and for Judas, and for Diarmaid of the Galls. "It's time for us to be saying the Rosary," says she. "Your father will tell you about Coilin Muirne some other night."

"Father," says I, and we going on our knees, "we should say a prayer for Coilin's soul this night."

"We'll do that, son," says my father kindly.

II

Sitting up one night, in the winter that was on us, my father told us the story of Muirne from start to finish. It's well I mind him in the firelight, a broad-shouldered man, a little stooped, his share of hair going grey, lines in his forehead, a sad look in his eyes. He was mending an old sail that night, and I was on my knees beside him in the name of helping him. My mother and my sisters were spinning frieze. Seaneen was stretched on his face on the floor, and he in grips of a book. 'Twas small the heed he gave to the same book, for it's the pastime he had, to be tickling the soles of my feet and taking an odd pinch out of my calves; but as my father stirred out in the story Sean gave over his trickery, and it is short till he was listening as interested as anyone. It would be hard not to listen to my father when he'd tell a story like that by the hearthside. He was a sweet storyteller. It's often I'd think there was music in his voice; a low, deep music like that in the bass of the organ in Tuam Cathedral.

Twenty years are gone, Coilin (says my father), since the night myself and Coilin Muirne (may God give him grace) and three or four others of the neighbours were in Neachtan's public-house in Uachtar Ard. There was a fair in the town the same day, and we were drinking a glass before taking the road home on ourselves. There were four or five men in it from Carrowroe and from the Joyce Country, and six or seven of the people of the town. There came a stranger in, a thin, black man that nobody knew. He called for a glass.

" Did ye hear, people," says he to us, and he drinking with us, " that the lord is to come home to-night? "

" What business has the devil here? " says someone.

" Bad work he's up to, as usual," says the black man. " He has settled to put seven families out of their holdings."

" Who's to be put out? " says one of us.

" Old Thomas O'Drinan from the Glen, —I'm told the poor fellow's dying, but it's on the roadside he'll die, if God hasn't him already ; a man of the O'Conaire's that lives in a cabin on this side of Loch Shindilla ; Manning from Snamh Bo ; two in Annagh-maan ; a woman at the head of the Island ; and Anthony O'Greelis from Lower Camus."

"Anthony's wife is heavy in child," says Cuimin O'Niadh.

"That won't save her, the creature," says the black man. "She's not the first woman out of this country that bore her child in a ditch-side of the road."

There wasn't a word out of anyone of us.

"What sort of men are ye?" says the black man,—"ye are not men, at all. I was born and raised in a countryside, and, my word to you, the men of that place wouldn't let the whole English army together throw out seven families on the road without them knowing the reason why. Are ye afraid of the man that's coming here to-night?"

"It's easy to talk," said Cuimin, "but what way can we stop the bodach?"

"Murder him this night," says a voice behind me. Everybody started. I myself turned round. It was Coilin Muirne that spoke. His two eyes were blazing in his head, a flame in his cheeks, and his head thrown high.

"A man that spoke that, whatever his name and surname," says the stranger. He went hither and gripped Coilin's hand. "Drink a glass with me," says he.

Coilin drank the glass. The others wouldn't speak.

"It's time for us to be shortening the road," says Cuimin, after a little spell.

We got a move on us. We took the road home. The night was dark. There was no wish for talk on any of us, at all. When we came to the head of the street Cuimin stood in the middle of the road.

"Where's Coilin Muirne?" says he.

We didn't feel him from us till Cuimin spoke. He wasn't in the company.

Myself went back to the public-house. Coilin wasn't in it. I questioned the pot-boy. He said that Coilin and the black man left the shop together five minutes after our going. I searched the town. There wasn't tale or tidings of Coilin anywhere. I left the town and I followed the other men. I hoped it might be that he'd be to find before me. He wasn't, nor the track of him.

It was very far in the night when we reached Glashaduff bridge. There was a light in Muirne's house. Muirne herself was standing in the door.

"God save you, men," says she, coming over to us. "Is Coilin with you?"

"He isn't, *muise*," says I. "He stayed behind us in Uachtar Ard."

"Did he sell?" says she.

"He did, and well," says I. "There's every chance that he'll stay in the town till morning. The night's black and cold in itself. Wouldn't it be as well for you to go in and lie down?"

"It's not worth my while," says she. "I'll **wait** up till he comes. May God hasten you."

We departed. There was, as it would be, a load on my heart. I was afraid that there was something after happening to Coilin. I had ill notions of that black man . . . I lay down on my bed after coming home, but I didn't sleep.

The next morning myself and your mother were eating breakfast, when the

latch was lifted from the door, and in comes
Cuimin O'Niadh. He could hardly draw
his breath.

"What's the news with you, man?"
says I.

"Bad news," says he. "The lord was
murdered last night. He was got on the
road a mile to the east of Uachtar Ard,
and a bullet through his heart. The
soldiers were in Muirne's house this morning on the track of Coilin, but he wasn't
there. He hasn't come home yet. It's
said it was he murdered the lord. You
mind the words he said last night?"

I leaped up, and out the door with me.
Down the road, and east to Muirne's house.
There was no one before me but herself.
The furniture of the house was this way
and that way, where the soldiers were
searching. Muirne got up when she saw
me in the door.

"Sean O'Conaire," says she, "for God's
pitiful sake, tell me where's my son? You
were along with him. Why isn't he
coming home to me?"

"Let you have patience, Muirne," says
I. "I'm going to Uachtar Ard after him."

THE KEENING WOMAN

I struck the road. Going in the street
of Uachtar Ard, I saw a great ruck of
people. The bridge and the street before
the chapel were black with people. People
were making on the spot from every art.
But, a thing that put terror on my heart,
there wasn't a sound out of that terrible
gathering,—only the eyes of every man
stuck in a little knot that was in the right-
middle of the crowd. Soldiers that were
in that little knot, black coats and red
coats on them, and guns and swords in
their hands ; and among the black coats
and red coats I saw a country boy, and
bawneens on him. Coilin Muirne that
was in it, and he in holds of the soldiers.
The poor boy's face was as white as my
shirt, but he had the beautiful head of him
lifted proudly, and it wasn't the head of a
coward, that head.

He was brought to the barracks, and that
crowd following him. He was taken to
Galway that night. He was put on his
trial the next month. It was sworn that
he was in the public-house that night. It
was sworn that the black man was discoursing on the landlords. It was sworn that

he said the lord would be coming that
night to throw the people out of their
holdings the next day. It was sworn that
Coilin Muirne was listening attentively to
him. It was sworn that Coilin said those
words, " Murder him this night," when
Cuimin O'Niadh said, " What way can we
stop the bodach?" It was sworn that the
black man praised him for saying those
words, that he shook hands with him,
that they drank a glass together. It was
sworn that Coilin remained in the shop
after the going of the Rossnageeragh people,
and that himself and the black man left
the shop together five minutes after that.
There came a peeler then, and he swore
he saw Coilin and the black man leaving
the town, and that it wasn't the Rossnageeragh road they took on themselves, but
the Galway road. At eight o'clock they
left the town. At half after eight a shot
was fired at the lord on the Galway road.
Another peeler swore he heard the report
of the shot. He swore he ran to the place,
and, closing up to the place, he saw two
men running away. A thin man one of
them was, and he dressed like a gentleman

would be. A country boy the other man was.

"What kind of clothes was the country boy wearing?" says the lawyer.

"A suit of bawneens," says the peeler.

"Is that the man you saw?" says the lawyer, stretching his finger towards Coilin.

"I would say it was."

"Do you swear it?"

The peeler didn't speak for a spell.

"Do you swear it?" says the lawyer again.

"I do," says the peeler. The peeler's face at that moment was whiter than the face of Coilin himself.

A share of us swore then that Coilin never fired a shot out of a gun; that he was a decent, kindly boy that wouldn't hurt a fly, if he had the power for it. The parish priest swore that he knew Coilin from the day he baptized him; that it was his opinion that he never committed a sin, and that he wouldn't believe from anyone at all that he would slay a man. It was no use for us. What good was our testimony against the testimony of the police? Judgment of death was given on Coilin.

His mother was present all that time. She didn't speak a word from start to finish, but her two eyes stuck in the two eyes of her son, and her two hands knitted under her shawl.

"He won't be hanged," says Muirne that night. "God promised me that he won't be hanged."

A couple of days after that we heard that Coilin wouldn't be hanged, that it's how his soul would be spared him on account of him being so young as he was, but that he'd be kept in gaol for the term of his life.

"He won't be kept," says Muirne. "O Jesus," she would say, "don't let them keep my son from me."

It's marvellous the patience that woman had, and the trust she had in the Son of God. It's marvellous the faith and the hope and the patience of women.

She went to the parish priest. She said to him that if he'd write to the people of Dublin, asking them to let Coilin out to her, it's certain he would be let out.

"They won't refuse you, Father," says she.

The priest said that there would be no

use at all in writing, that no heed would b.
paid to his letter, but that he himself would
go to Dublin and that he would speak with
the great people, and that, maybe, some good
might come out of it. He went. Muirne
was full-sure her son would be home to her
by the end of a week or two. She readied
the house before him. She put lime on it
herself, inside and outside. She set two
neighbours to put a new thatch on it. She
spun the makings of a new suit of clothes
for him; she dyed the wool with her own
hands; she brought it to the weaver, and
she made the suit when the frieze came
home.

We thought it long while the priest was
away. He wrote a couple of times to the
master, but there was nothing new in the
letters. He was doing his best, he said, but
he wasn't succeeding too well. He was
going from person to person, but it's not
much satisfaction anybody was giving him.
It was plain from the priest's letters that he
hadn't much hope he'd be able to do anything. None of us had much hope, either.
But Muirne didn't lose the wonderful trust
she had in God.

" The priest will bring my son home with him," she used say.

There was nothing making her anxious but fear that she wouldn't have the new suit ready before Coilin's coming. But it was finished at last; she had everything ready, repair on the house, the new suit laid on a chair before the fire,—and still no word of the priest.

" Isn't it Coilin will be glad when he sees the comfort I have in the house," she would say. "Isn't it he will look spruce going the road to Mass of a Sunday, and that suit on him!"

It's well I mind the evening the priest came home. Muirne was waiting for him since morning, the house cleaned up, and the table laid.

" Welcome home," she said, when the priest came in. She was watching the door, as she would be expecting someone else to come in. But the priest closed the door after him.

" I thought that it's with yourself he'd come, Father," says Muirne. " But, sure, it's the way he wouldn't like to come on the priest's car. He was shy like that always, the creature."

"Oh, poor Muirne," says the priest, holding her by the two hands, "I can't conceal the truth from you. He's not coming, at all. I didn't succeed in doing anything. They wouldn't listen to me."

Muirne didn't say a word. She went over and she sat down before the fire. The priest followed her and laid his hand on her shoulder.

"Muirne," says he, like that.

"Let me be, Father, for a little while," says she. "May God and His Mother reward you for what you've done for me. But leave me to myself for a while. I thought you'd bring him home to me, and it's a great blow on me that he hasn't come."

The priest left her to herself. He thought he'd be no help to her till the pain of that blow would be blunted.

The next day Muirne wasn't to be found. Tale or tidings no one had of her. Word nor wisdom we never heard of her till the end of a quarter. A share of us thought that it's maybe out of her mind the creature went, and a lonely death to come on her in the hollow of some mountain, or drowning

in a boghole. The neighbours searched
the hills round about, but her track wasn't
to be seen.

One evening myself was digging potatoes
in the garden, when I saw a solitary woman
making on me up the road. A tall, thin
woman. Her head well-set. A great
walk under her. " If Muirne ni Fhiannachta is living," says I to myself, " it's she
that's in it." 'Twas she, and none else.
Down with me to the road.

" Welcome home, Muirne," says I to
her. " Have you any news ? "

" I have, then," says she, " and good
news. I went to Galway. I saw the
Governor of the gaol. He said to me that
he wouldn't be able to do a taste, that it's
the Dublin people would be able to let him
out of gaol, if his letting-out was to be got.
I went off to Dublin. O, Lord, isn't it
many a hard, stony road I walked, isn't it
many a fine town I saw before I came to
Dublin ? ' Isn't it a great country, Ireland
is ? ' I used say to myself every evening
when I'd be told I'd have so many miles to
walk before I'd see Dublin. But, great
thanks to God and to the Glorious Virgin, I

walked in on the street of Dublin at last, one cold, wet evening. I found a lodging. The morning of the next day I enquired for the Castle. I was put on the way. I went there. They wouldn't let me in at first, but I was at them till I got leave of talk with some man. He put me on to another man, a man that was higher than himself. He sent me to another man. I said to them all I wanted was to see the Lord Lieutenant of the Queen. I saw him at last. I told him my story. He said to me that he couldn't do anything. I gave my curse to the Castle of Dublin, and out the door with me. I had a pound in my pocket. I went aboard a ship, and the morning after I was in Liverpool of the English. I walked the long roads of England from Liverpool to London. When I came to London I asked knowledge of the Queen's Castle. I was told. I went there. They wouldn't let me in. I went there every day, hoping that I'd see the Queen coming out. After a week I saw her coming out. There were soldiers and great people about her. I went over to the Queen before she went in to her coach.

THE KEENING WOMAN

There was a paper, a man in Dublin wrote
for me, in my hand.   An officer seized me.
The Queen spoke to him, and he freed me
from him.   I spoke to the Queen.   She
didn't understand me.   I stretched the paper
to her.   She gave the paper to the officer,
and he read it.   He wrote certain words
on the paper, and he gave it back to me.
The Queen spoke to another woman that
was along with her.   The woman drew out
a crown piece and gave it to me.   I gave
her back the crown piece, and I said that
it's not silver I wanted, but my son.   They
laughed.   It's my opinion they didn't
understand me.   I showed them the paper
again.   The officer laid his finger on the
words he was after writing.   I curtseyed
to the Queen and went off with me.   A
man read for me the words the officer wrote.
It's what was in it, that they would write
to me about Coilin without delay.   I struck
the road home then, hoping that, maybe,
there would be a letter before me.   "Do
you think, Sean," says Muirne, finishing
her story, "has the priest any letter?
There wasn't a letter at all in the house
before me coming out the road; but I'm

thinking it's to the priest they'd send the letter, for it's a chance the great people might know him."

" I don't know did any letter come," says I. " I would say there didn't, for if there did the priest would be telling us."

" It will be here some day yet," says Muirne. " I'll go in to the priest, anyhow, and I'll tell him my story."

In the road with her, and up the hill to the priest's house. I saw her going home again that night, and the darkness falling. It's wonderful how she was giving it to her footsoles, considering what she suffered of distress and hardship for a quarter.

A week went by. There didn't come any letter. Another week passed. No letter came. The third week, and still no letter. It would take tears out of the grey stones to be looking at Muirne, and the anxiety that was on her. It would break your heart to see her going in the road to the priest every morning. We were afraid to speak to her about Coilin. We had evil notions. The priest had evil notions. He said to us one day that he heard from another priest in Galway that it's not more

222

than well Coilin was, that it's greatly the
prison was preying on his health, that he
was going back daily. That story wasn't
told to Muirne.

One day myself had business with the
priest, and I went in to him. We were
conversing in the parlour when we heard a
person's footstep on the street outside.
Never a knock on the house-door, or on
the parlour-door, but in into the room with
Muirne ni Fhiannachta, and a letter in her
hand. It's with trouble she could talk.

" A letter from the Queen, a letter from
the Queen!" says she.

The priest took the letter. He opened
it. I noticed that his hand was shaking,
and he opening it. There came the colour
of death in his face after reading it. Muirne
was standing out opposite him, her two
eyes blazing in her head, her mouth half open.

" What does she say, Father?" says she.
" Is she sending him home to me?"

" It's not from the Queen this letter came,
Muirne," says the priest, speaking slowly,
like as there would be some impediment on
him, " but from the Governor of the gaol
in Dublin."

" And what does he say ?   Is he sending
him home to me ? "

The priest didn't speak for a minute.   It
seemed to me that he was trying to mind
certain words, and the words, as you would
say, going from him.

" Muirne," says he at last, " he says that
poor Coilin died yesterday."

At the hearing of those words, Muirne
burst a-laughing.   The like of such laughter
I never heard.   That laughter was ringing
in my ears for a month after that.   She
made a couple of terrible screeches of
laughter, and then she fell in a faint on
the floor.

She was fetched home, and she was on
her bed for a half year.   She was out of
her mind all that time.   She came to herself at long last, and no person at all would
think there was a thing the matter with
her,—only the delusion that her son isn't
returned home yet from the fair of Uachtar
Ard.   She does be expecting him always,
standing or sitting in the door half the day,
and everything ready for his home-coming.
She doesn't understand that there's any
change on the world since that night. " That's

the reason, Coilin," says my father to me,
that she didn't know the railway was
coming as far as Burnt House. Times
she remembers herself, and she starts keening
like you saw her. 'Twas herself that made
yon keen you heard from her. May God
comfort her, says my father," putting an
end to his story.

"And daddy," says I, "did any letter
come from the Queen after that?"

"There didn't, nor the colour of one."

"Do you think, daddy, was it Coilin that
killed the lord?"

"I know it wasn't," says my father. "If
it was he'd acknowledge it. I'm as certain
as I'm living this night that it's the black
man killed the lord. I don't say that poor
Coilin wasn't present."

"Was the black man ever caught?" says
my sister.

"He wasn't, *muise*," says my father.
"Little danger on him."

"Where did he belong, the black man,
do you think, daddy?" says I.

"I believe, before God," says my father,
"that it's a peeler from Dublin Castle was
in it. Cuimin O'Niadh saw a man very like

225   Q

IOSAGAN

Old Matthias was sitting beside his door. Anyone going the road would think that it was an image of stone or of marble was in it—that, or a dead person—for he couldn't believe that a living man could stay so calm, so quiet as that. He had his head high and an ear on him listening. It's many a musical sound there was to listen to, for the person who'd have heed on them. Old Matthias heard the roar of the waves on the rocks, and the murmur of the stream flowing down and over the stones. He heard the screech of the heron-crane from the high, rocky shore, and the lowing of the cows from the pasture, and the bright laughter of the children from the green. But it wasn't to any of these he was listening that attentively—though all of them were sweet to him—but to the clear sound of the bell for Mass that was coming to him on the wind in the morning stillness.

All the people were gathered into Mass. Old Matthias saw them going past, in ones

and twos, or in little groups. The boys
were running and leaping. The girls were
chattering merrily. The women were
conversing in low tones. The men were
silent. Like this, they'd travel the road
every Sunday. Like this, Old Matthias
would sit on his chair watching them till
they'd go out of sight. They went past
him this morning as usual. The old man
remained looking at them till there was an
end to the noise and the commotion, till
the last group cleared the top of the church
hill, till there was nothing to be seen but
a long, straight road stretching out, and it
white, till there were none to be found in
the village but an odd old person in his bed,
or children tricking on the green, and himself sitting beside his door.

Old Matthias would not go to the chapel.
He hadn't heard " the sweet Mass " for
over three score years. He was a strong,
active youth the last time he blessed himself before the people, and now he was a
withered, done old man, his share of hair
grey-white, furrows in his brow, his
shoulders bent. He hadn't bent his knee
before God for the length of those three

score years ; he hadn't put a prayer to his
Creator ; he hadn't given thanks to his
Saviour. A man apart, Old Matthias
was.

Nobody knew why he wouldn't go to
Mass. People said that he didn't believe
there was a God in it. Other people said
that he committed some terrible sin at the
start of his life, and when the priest wouldn't
give him absolution in confession, that a
rage of anger came on him, and he swore
an oath that he wouldn't touch priest or
chapel while he was living again. Other
people said—but this was said only in a
whisper by the fireside when the old people
would be yarning by themselves after the
children had gone asleep—these said that
he sold his soul to a certain Great Man
that he met once on the top of Cnoc-a'-
daimh, and that this person wouldn't allow
him to frequent the Mass. I don't know
is it true or lying these stories are, but I do
know that old Matthias wasn't seen at God's
Mass in the memory of the oldest person
in the village. Cuimin O'Niadh—an old
man that got death a couple of years before
this in his ninetieth year—said that he

himself saw him there when he was a lump
of a lad.

It wasn't thought that Old Matthias was
a bad character.   He was a man as honest,
as simple, as natural as you would meet in
a day's walking.   There wasn't ever heard
out of his mouth but the good word.   He
had no delight in drink or in company, no
wish for gold or for property.   He was
poor, but it's often he shared with people
that were poorer than he.   He had pity for
the infirm.   He had mercy for the wretched.
Other men had honour and esteem for him.
The women, the children, and the animals
loved him ; and he had love for them and
for everything that was generous and of
clean heart.

Old Matthias liked women's talk better
than men's talk.   But he liked the talk of
boys and girls still better than the talk of
men or women.   He used say that the
women were more discerning than the men,
and that the children were more discerning
than either of them.   It's along with the
young folk he would spend the best part of
his idle time.   He would sit with them in
a corner of the house, telling them stories,

or getting stories out of them. They were
wonderful, his share of stories. He had
the " Adventures of the Grey Horse " in
grandest way in the world. He was the
one old body in the village who had
the story of the " Hen-Harrier and the
Wren," properly. Isn't it he would put
fright on the children, and he reciting " *Fú
Fá Féasóg*" (The Two-Headed Giant), and
isn't it he would take the laughs out of
them discoursing on the doings of the
piper in the Snail's Castle ! And the songs
he had ! He could coax an ailing child
asleep with his :

" Shoheen, sho, and sleep, my pet ;
   The fairies are out walking the glen !"

or he could put the full of a house of
children in fits of laughter with his :

" Hi diddle dum, the cat and his mother,
   That went to Galway riding a drake !"

And isn't it he had the funny old ranns ; and
the hard, difficult questions ; and the fine
riddles ! As for games, where was the
person, man, woman, or child could keep
" *Lúrabóg, Lárabóg*," or " *An Bhuidhean*

233

Bhalbh" (The Dumb Band) going with him !

In the fine time it's on the side of the hill, or walking the bog, you'd see Old Matthias and his little playmates, he explaining to them the way of life of the ants and of the woodlice, or inventing stories about the hedgehog and the red squirrel. Another time to them boating, the old man with an oar, some little wee boy with another one, and maybe a young girl steering. It's often the people who'd be working near the strand would hear the shouts of joy of the children coming to them from the harbour-mouth, or, it might be, Old Matthias's voice, and he saying :

" Oró ! my curragheen O !
And óró ! my little boat !"

or something like it.

There used come fear on a share of the mothers at times, and they'd say to each other that they oughtn't let their children spend that much time with Old Matthias,— "a man that frequents neither clergy nor Mass." Once a woman of them laid bare these thoughts to Father Sean. It's what the priest said :

"Don't meddle with the poor children,"
says he. "They couldn't be in better
company."

"But they tell me he doesn't believe in
God, Father."

"There's many a saint in heaven to-day
that didn't believe in God some time of his
life. And, whisper here. If Old Matthias
hasn't love for God—a thing that neither
you nor I know—it's wonderful the love he
has for the cleanest and most beautiful thing
that God created,—the shining soul of
the child. Our Saviour Himself and the
most glorious saints in heaven had the same
love for them. How do we know that it
isn't the children that will draw Old Matthias
to the knee of our Saviour yet?"

And the story was left like that.

On this Sunday morning the old man
remained listening till the bell for Mass
stopped ringing. When there was an end
to it he gave a sigh, as the person would
that would be weary and sorrowful, and he
turned to the group of boys that were sport-
ing themselves on the plot of grass—the
"green" Old Matthias would call it—at
the cross-roads. Old Matthias knew every

curly-headed, bare-footed child of them.
He liked no pastime at all better than
to be sitting there watching them and
listening to them. He was counting them,
seeing which of his friends were in it and
which of them were gone to Mass with the
grown people, when he noticed among them
a child he never saw before. A little, brown
boy, with a white coat on him, like was on
every other boy, and he without shoes or
cap, as is the custom with the children of
the West. The face of this boy was as
bright as the sun, and it seemed to Old
Matthias that there were, as it would be,
rays of light coming from his head. The
sun shining on his share of hair, maybe.

There was wonder on the old man at
seeing this child, for he hadn't heard that
there were any strangers after coming to the
village. He was on the point of going
over and questioning one of the little lads
about him, when he heard the stir and
chatter of the people coming home from
Mass. He didn't feel the time slipping by
him while his mind was on the tricks of the
boys. Some of the people saluted him going
past, and he saluted them. When he gave

an eye on the group of boys again, the strange boy wasn't among them.

The Sunday after that, Old Matthias was sitting beside his door, as usual. The people were gathered west to Mass. The young folk were running and throwing jumps on the green. Running and throwing jumps along with them was the strange child. Matthias looked at him for a long time, for he gave the love of his heart to him on account of the beauty of his person and the brightness of his countenance. At last he called over one of the little boys:

" Who's yon boy I see among you for a fortnight back, Coilin ? " says he—" he there with the brown head on him,—but have a care that it's not reddish-fair he is : I don't know is it dark or fair he is, and the way the sun is burning on him. Do you see him now—that one that's running towards us ? "

" That's Iosagan," says the little lad.

" Iosagan ? "

" That's the name he gives himself."

" Who are his people ? "

" I don't know, but he says his father's a king."

237

" Where does he live? "

" He never told us that, but he says that it's not far from us his house is."

" Does he be along with you often? "

" Aye, when we do be spending time to ourselves like this. But he goes from us when a grown person is present. Look! he's gone already! "

The old man looked, and there was no one in it but the boys he knew. The child, the little boy called Iosagan, was missing. The same moment, the noise and bustle of the people were heard returning from Mass.

The next Sunday everything fell out exactly as it fell on the two Sundays before that. The people gathered west as usual, and the old man and the children were left by themselves in the village. The heart of Old Matthias gave a leap in his middle when he saw the Holy Child among them again.

He rose. He went over and he stood near Him. After a time, standing without a move, he stretched his two hands towards Him, and he spoke in a low voice:

" Iosagan! "

IOSAGAN

The Child heard him, and He came towards him, running.

"Come here and sit on my knee for a little while, Iosagan."

The Child put His hand in the thin, knuckly hand of the old man, and they travelled side by side across the road. Old Matthias sat on his chair, and drew Iosagan to his breast.

"Where do You live, Iosagan?" says he, speaking low always.

"Not far from this My House is. Why don't you come on a visit to Me?"

"I'd be afraid in a royal house. It's told me that Your Father's a King."

"He is High-King of the World. But there is no need for you to be afraid of Him. He is full of mercy and love."

"I fear I haven't kept His law."

"Ask forgiveness of Him. I and My Mother will make intercession for you."

"It's a pity I didn't see You before this, Iosagan. Where were You from me?"

"I was here always. I do be travelling the roads, and walking the hills, and ploughing the waves. I do be among the people when they gather into My House. I do be

239

among the children they do leave behind them playing on the street."

" I was too timid—or too proud—to go into Your House, Iosagan ; but I found You among the children."

" There isn't any time or place that children do be amusing themselves that I am not along with them. Times they see Me ; other times they do not see Me."

" I never saw You till lately."

" The grown people do be blind."

" And it has been granted me to see You, Iosagan ? "

" My Father gave Me leave to show Myself to you, because you loved His little children."

The voices were heard of the people returning from Mass.

" I must go now from you."

" Let me kiss the border of Your coat, Iosagan."

" Kiss it."

" Shall I see You again ? "

" You will."

" When ? "

" This night."

With that word He was gone.

IOSAGAN

"I will see Him this night!" says Old Matthias, and he going into the house.

.   .   .   .

The night came wet and stormy. The great waves were heard breaking with a booming roar against the strand. The trees round the chapel were swaying and bending with the strength of the wind. (The chapel is on a little hill that falls down with a slope to the sea.) Father Sean was on the point of closing his book and saying his Rosary when he heard a noise, as it would be somebody knocking at the door. He listened for a spell. He heard the noise again. He rose from the fire, went to the door, and opened it. A little boy was standing on the door-flag—a boy the priest didn't mind ever to have seen before. He had a white coat on him, and he without shoes or cap. The priest thought that there were rays of light shining from his countenance, and about his head. The moon that was shining on his brown, comely head, it's like.

"Who have I here?" says Father Sean.

"Put on you as quickly as you're able,

Father, and strike east to the house of
Old Matthias. He is in the mouths of
death."

The priest didn't want the second word.

"Sit here till I'm ready," says he. But when
he came back, the little messenger was gone.

Father Sean struck the road, and he didn't
take long to finish the journey, though the
wind was against him, and it raining heavily.
There was a light in Old Matthias's house
before him. He took the latch from the
door, and went in.

"Who is this coming to me?" says a voice
from the old man's bed.

"The priest."

"I'd like to speak to you, Father. Sit
here beside me." The voice was feeble, and
the words came slowly from him.

The priest sat down, and heard Old
Matthias's story from beginning to end.
Whatever secret was in the old body's
heart it was laid bare to the servant of God
there in the middle of the night. When
the confession was over, Old Matthias
received communion, and he was anointed.

"Who told you that I was wanting you,
Father?" says he in a weak, low voice, when

everything was done. "I was praying God that you'd come, but I hadn't any messenger to send for you."

"But, sure, you did send a messenger to me?" says the priest, and great wonder on him.

"I didn't."

"You didn't? But a little boy came, and he knocked at my door, and he said to me that you were wanting my help!"

The old man sat up straight in the bed. There was a flashing in his eyes.

"What sort was the little boy was in it, Father?"

"A gentle little boy, with a white coat on him."

"Did you take notice was there a haze of light about his head?"

"I did, and it put great wonder on me."

Old Matthias looked up, there came a smile on his mouth, and he stretched out his two arms:

"Iosagan!" says he.

With that word, he fell back on the bed. The priest went hither to him softly, and closed his eyes.

243

THE PRIEST

It's in yon little house you see in the glen
below you, and you going down the road
from Gortmore to Inver, that my Priest
lives. Himself and his mother, and his little
sister, and his little, small, wee brother,—
those are the family in it. The father died
before Taimeen, the youngest child of them,
was born. There's no time I do be in
Rossnageeragh but I spend an evening or
two along with them, for the Priest and
Maireen (the little sister) and Taimeen are
the dearest friends I have. A soft, youngish-
looking woman the Priest's mother is; she's
a bit headstrong, maybe, but if she is itself
she's as kind-hearted a woman as is living,
after that. 'Twas she told me this story
one evening that I was on a visit to her.
She was washing the Priest, meanwhile,
before the fire: a big tub of water laid on
the floor beside her, the Priest and his share
of clothes stripped from him, and she rubbing and scrubbing every inch of his body.
I have my doubts that this work agreed too

247

well with the Priest, for now and again he'd
let a screech out of him. With every
screech his mother would give him a little
slap, and after that she'd kiss him. It's
hard for a mother to keep her hand off a
child when she has him bare ; and 'twould
be harder than that for a mother, as loving
as this mother, to keep her mouth from a
wee, red moutheen as sweet as Paraig's
(Paraig's my Priest's name, you know). I
ought to say that the Priest was only eight
years old yet. He was a lovely picture,
standing there, and the firelight shining on
his well-knit body and on his curly head,
and dancing in his grey, laughing eyes.
When I think on Paraig, it's that way I see
him before me, standing on the floor in the
brightening of the fire.

But in regard to the story. About a
year before this it is it fell out. Nora (the
mother) was working about the house.
Maireen and Taimeen were amusing themselves on the floor. " *Fromsó Framsó* " they
had going on. Maireen was trying to teach
the words to Taimeen, a thing that was
failing on her, for Taimeen hadn't any talk
yet. You know the words, I suppose ?—

they're worth learning, for there's true
poetry in them:

> "*Fromsó Framsó,*——
> A woman dancing,
> That would make sport,
> That would drink ale,
> That would be in time
> Here in the morning!"

Nora wanted a can of water to make tea.
It was supper-time.

"Where's Paraig, Maireen?" says she.
"He's lost this half-hour."

"He went into the room, mameen."

"Paraig!" says the mother, calling
loudly.

Not a word from within.

"Do you hear, Paraig?"

Never a word.

"What's wrong with the boy? Paraig,
I say!" says she, as loud as it was in her
head.

"I'll be out presently, mama," says a
voice from the room.

"Hurry with you, son. It's tea-time,
and devil a tear of water have I in the
house."

249

Paraig came out of the room.

"You're found at last. Push on down with you,—but what's this? Where did you get that shirt, or why is it on you? What were you doing?"

Paraig was standing in the door, like a stake. A shirt was fastened on him over his little coat. He looked down on himself. His face was red-burning to the ears.

"I forgot to take it off me, mama," says he.

"Why is it on you at all?"

"Sport I was having."

"Take it off you this minute! The rod you want, yourself and your sport!"

Paraig took off the shirt without a word and left it back in the room.

"Brush down to the well now and get a can of water for me, like a pet." Nora already regretted that she spoke as harshly as that. It's a woman's anger that isn't lasting.

Paraig took the can and whipped off with it. Michileen Enda, a neighbour's boy, came in while he was out.

"It beats me, Michileen," says Nora, after a spell, "to make out what Paraig does

be doing in that room the length of the
evening. No sooner has he his dinner
eaten every day than he clears off in there,
and he's lost till supper-time."

" Some sport he does have on foot," says
Michileen.

" That's what he says himself. But it's
not in the house a lad like him ought to be
stuck on a fine evening, but outside in the
air, tearing away."

" ' A body's will is his delight,' " says
Michileen, reddening his pipe.

" One apart is Paraig, anyhow," says
Nora. " He's the most contrary son you
ever saw. Times, three people wouldn't
watch him, and other times you wouldn't
feel him in the house."

Paraig came in at this, and no more was
said on the question. He didn't steal away
this time, but instead of that he sat down on
the floor, playing " *Fromsó Framsó* " with
Maireen and Taimeen.

.   .   .   .   .   .

The dinner was on the table when Paraig
came home from school the next evening.
He ate his share of stirabout and he drank

251

his noggin of milk, thankfully and with blessing. As soon as he had eaten and drunk, he took his satchel of books and west with him into the room, as was his habit.

The mother didn't let on that she was giving any heed to him. But, after a couple of minutes, she opened the door of the room quietly, and stuck the tip of her nose inside. Paraig didn't notice her, but she had a view of everything that was going on in the room.

It was a queer sight. Paraig was standing beside the table and he dressed in the shirt again. Outside of this, and back over his shoulders, he was fixing a red bodice of his mother's, that she had hanging on the wall. When he had this arranged properly, he took out the biggest book he had in his satchel—the " Second Book " it was, I believe—he opened it, and laid it before him on the table, propped against the looking-glass.

It's then began the antics in earnest. Paraig stood out opposite the table, bent his knee, blessed himself, and began praying loudly. It's not well Nora was able to understand him, but, as she thought, he had Latin and Gaelic mixed through other, and

an odd word that wasn't like Latin or Gaelic.
Once, it seemed to her, she heard the words
" *Fromsó Framsó*," but she wasn't sure.
Whatever wonder was on Nora at this, it
was seven times greater the wonder was on
her when she saw Paraig genuflecting, beating his breast, kissing the table, letting on
he was reading Latin prayers out of the
" Second Book," and playing one trick odder
than another. She didn't know rightly
what he was up to, till he turned round and
said :

" *Dominus vobiscum !* "

" God save us ! " says she to herself when
she saw this. " He's pretending that he's
a priest and he reading Mass! That's the
Mass vestment he's wearing, and the little
Gaelic book is the book of the Mass ! "

It's no exaggeration to say that Nora
was scared. She came back to the kitchen
and sat before the fire. She didn't know
what she ought to do. She was between
two advices, which of them would be seem-
liest for her—to put Paraig across her knee
and give him a good whipping, or to go
on her two knees before him and beg his
blessing !

" How do I know," says she to herself,
" that it's not a terrible sin for me to let him
make a mimic of the priest like that?   But
how do I know, after that, that it's not a
saint out of heaven I have in the house?
And, sure, it would be a dreadful sin to lay
hand on a saint!   May God forgive it to
me, it's often I laid the track of my fingers
on him already!   I don't know either way.
I'm in a strait, surely!"   Nora didn't sleep
a wink that night with putting this question
through other.

The next morning, as soon as Paraig was
cleared off to school, Nora put the lock on the
door, left the two young children under the
care of Michileen's mother, and struck
the road to Rossnageeragh.   She didn't stop
till she came to the parish priest's house
and told her story to Father Ronan from
start to finish.   The priest only smiled, but
Nora was with him till she drew a promise
from him that he'd take the road out to her
that evening.   She whipped home then,
satisfied.

The priest didn't fail her.   He struck in
to her in the evening.   Timely enough,
Paraig was in the room " reading Mass."

"On your life, don't speak, Father!"
says Nora. "He's within."

The two stole over on their tiptoes to the
room door. They looked inside. Paraig
was dressed in the shirt and bodice, exactly
as he was the day before that, and he praying piously. The priest stood a spell looking
at him.

At last my lad turned round, and setting
his face towards the people, as it would be :

"*Orate, fratres,*" says he, out loud.

While this was saying, he saw his mother
and the priest in the door. He reddened,
and stood without a stir.

"Come here to me," says Father Ronan.

Paraig came over timidly.

"What's this you have going on?" says
the priest.

"I was reading Mass, Father," says Paraig.
He said this much shyly, but it was plain he
didn't think that he had done anything out of
the way—and, sure, it's not much he had.
But poor Nora was on a tremble with
fear.

"Don't be too hard on him, Father,"
says she. "He's only young."

The priest laid his hand lightly on the

255

white head of the little lad, and he spoke
gently and kindly to him.

"You're too young yet, Paraigeen," says
he, "to be a priest, and it's not granted to
anyone but to God's priest to say the Mass.
But whisper here to me. Would you like
to be serving Mass on Sunday?"

Paraig's eyes lit up and his cheek reddened
again, not with shyness this time but with
sheer delight.

"*Ora*, I would, Father," says he; "I'd
like nothing at all better."

"That will do," says the priest. "I see
you have some of the prayers already."

"But, Father, *a mhuirnín*"—says Nora,
and stopped like that, suddenly.

"What's on you now?" says the priest.

"Breeches nor brogues he hasn't worn
yet!" says she. "I think it early to put
breeches on him till —"

The priest burst out laughing.

"I never heard," says he, "that there
was call for breeches. We'll put a little
cassock out over his coat, and I warrant it'll
fit him nicely. As for shoes, we've a pair
that Martin the Fisherman left behind him
when he went to Clifden. We'll dress you

BARBARA

Barbara wasn't too well-favoured, the best day she was. Anybody would admit that much. The first cause of it,—she was purblind. You'd say, to look at her, she was one-eyed. Brideen never gave in that she was, however. Once when another little girl said, out of sheer spite on them both, that Barbara had only "one blind little eye, like the tailor's cat," Brideen said angrily that Barbara had her two eyes as good as anybody, but it's how she'd have one eye shut, for the one was enough for her (let it be blind), to do her share of work. However it was, it couldn't be hidden that she was bald ; and I declare a bald head isn't a nice thing in a young woman. Another thing, she was a dummy ; or it would be more correct for me to say, that she didn't ever speak with anybody, but with Brideen only. If Brideen told truth, she had a tasty tongue of Irish, and her share of thoughts were the loveliest in the world. It's not well she could walk, for she was one-legged, and that one leg itself broken. She had two legs on a time, but the dog ate one of them, and the other was broken where she fell from the top of the dresser.

But who's Barbara, say you, or who's Brideen? Brideen is the little girl, or, as she'd say herself, the little slip of a woman, that lives in the house next the master's,— on the left-hand side, I think, going up the road. It's likely you know her now? If you don't, I can't help you. I never heard who her people were, and she herself said to me that her father has ne'er a name but "Daddy." As for Barbara,—well, it's as good for me to tell you her adventures and travels from start to finish.

THE ADVENTURES OF BARBARA HERE.

One day when Brideen's mother got up, she gave their breakfasts to Brideen and to her father, to the dog, to the little cat, to the calves, to the hens, to the geese, to the ducks, and to the little robin redbreast that would come to the door at breakfast-time every morning. When she had that much done, she ate her own breakfast. Then she began readying herself for the road.

Brideen was sitting on her own little stool without a word out of her, but she putting the eyes through her mother. At long last she spoke:

"Is mama going from Brideen?"

"She's not, *a stóir*. Mama will come again in the evening. She's going to Galway."

"Is Brideen going there, too?"

"She's not, *a chuid*. The road's too long, and my little girl would be tired. She'll stay at home making sport for herself, like a good little girl would. Won't she stay?"

"She will."

"She won't run out on the street?"

"She won't."

"Daddy'll come in at dinner-time, and ye'll have a meal together. Give mama a kiss, now."

The kiss was given, and the mother was going. Brideen started up.

"Mama!"

"What is it *a rúin*?"

"Won't you bring home a fairing to Brideen?"

" I will, *a chuid*.   A pretty fairing."

The mother went off, and Brideen remained contented at home.   She sat down on her little stool.   The dog was curled before the fire, and he snoring.   Brideen woke him up, and put a whisper in his ear :

" Mama will bring home a fairing to Brideen ! "

" Wuff ! " says the dog, and went asleep to himself again.   Brideen knew that " Wuff ! " was the same as " Good news ! "

The little cat was sitting on the hearth. Brideen lifted it in her two arms, rubbed its face to her cheeks, and put a whisper in its ear :

" Mama will bring home a fairing to Brideen ! "

" Mee-ow ! " says the little cat.   Brideen knew that " Mee-ow ! " was the same as " Good news ! "

She laid the little cat from her, and went about the house singing to herself.   She made a little song as follows :

" O little dog, and O little dog !
Sleep a while till my mama comes !
O little cat, and O little cat !

Be purring till she comes home !
O little dog, and O little cat !
At the fair O ! my mama is,
But she'll come again in the little
    evening O !
And she'll bring home a fairing
    with her !"

She tried to teach this song to the dog,
but it's greater the wish the dog had for
sleep than for music. She tried to teach
it to the little cat, but the little cat thought
its own purring sweeter. When her father
came in at midday, nothing would do her
but to say this song to him, and make him
to learn it by heart.

The mother returned home before evening. The first word Brideen said was :

"Did you bring the fairing with you,
mama ?"

"I did, *a chuisle.*"

"What did you bring with you ?"

"Guess !" The mother was standing
in the middle of the floor. She had her
bag laid on the floor, and her hands behind
her.

"Sweets ?"

" No ! "

" A sugar cake ? "

" No, *muise* !   I have a sugar cake in my bag, but that's not the fairing,"

" A pair of stockings ? "   Brideen never wore shoes or stockings, and she had been long coveting them.

" No, indeed !   You're too young for stockings a little while yet."

" A prayer book ? "   There's no need for me to say that Brideen wasn't able to read (for she hadn't put in a day at school in her life), but she thought she was.   " A prayer book ? " says she.

" Not at all ! "

" What is it, then ? "

" Look ! "

The mother spread out her two hands, and what did she lay bare but a little doll ! A little wooden doll that was bald, and it purblind ; but its two cheeks were as red as a berry, and there was a smile on its mouth. Anybody who'd have an affection for dolls, he would give affection and love to it. Brideen's eyes lit up with joy.

" *Ora*, isn't it pretty !   *Ara*, mama, heart, where did you get it ?   *Ora ó !*   I'll have

266

a child of my very own now,—a child of
my very owneen own ! Brideen will have
a child ! ”

She snatched the little doll, and she squeezed
it to her heart. She kissed its little bald
head, and its two red cheeks. She kissed
its little mouth, and its little snub nose.
Then she remembered herself, raised her
head, and says she to her mother :

“ Kith ! ” (like that Brideen would say
“ Kiss.”)

The mother stooped down till the little
girl kissed her. Then she must kiss the
little doll. The father came in at that
moment, and he was made do the same.

There wasn't a thing making Brideen
anxious that evening but what name she'd
christen the doll. Her mother praised
“ Molly ” for it, and her father thought
the name “ Peggy ” would be apt. But
none of these were grand enough, it seemed
to Brideen.

“ Why was I called Brideen, daddy ? ”
says she after supper.

“ The old women said that you were like
your uncle Padraic, and since we couldn't
christen you ‘ Padraic,’ you were christened

'Brigid,' as that, we thought, was the thing nearest it."

"Do you think is she here" (the doll), "like my uncle Padraic, daddy?"

"O, not like a bit. Your uncle Padraic is fair-haired,—and, I believe, he has a beard on him now."

"Who's she like, then?"

"*Muise*, 'twould be hard to say, girl!— 'twould be hard, that."

Brideen meditated for a while. Her father was stripping her clothes from her in front of the fire during this time, for it was time for her to be going to sleep. When she was stripped, she went on her knees, put her two little hands together, and she began like this:

"O Jesus Christ, bless us and save us! O Jesus Christ, bless daddy and mama and Brideen, and keep us safe and well from accident, and from the harm of the year, if it is the will of my Saviour. O God, bless my uncle Padraic that's now in America, and my Aunt Barbara —." She stopped, suddenly, and put a shout of joy out of her.

"I have it! I have it, daddy!" says she.

" What have you, love ?   Wait till you finish your share of prayers."

" My Aunt Barbara ! She's like my Aunt Barbara !"

" Who's like your Aunt Barbara ? "

" The little doll ! That's the name I'll give her ! Barbara !"

The father let a great shout of laughter before he remembered that the prayers weren't finished. Brideen didn't laugh, at all, but followed on like this :

" O God, bless my Uncle Padaric that's now in America, and my Aunt Barbara, and (this is an addition she put to it herself), and bless my own little Barbara, and keep her from mortal sin ! Amen, O Lord !"

The father burst laughing again. Brideen looked at him, and wonder on her.

" Brush off, now, and in into your bed with you !" says he, as soon as he could speak for the laughing. " And don't forget Barbara !" says he.

" Little fear !" West with her into the room, and into the bed with her with a leap. Be sure she didn't forget Barbara.

From that night out Brideen wouldn't

go to sleep, for gold nor for silver, without
Barbara being in the bed with her. She
wouldn't sit to take food without Barbara
sitting beside her. She wouldn't go out
making fun to herself without Barbara
being along with her. One Sunday that
her mother brought her with her to Mass,
Brideen wasn't satisfied till Barbara was
brought, too. A neighbour woman wouldn't
come in visiting, but Barbara would be
introduced to her. One day that the priest
struck in to them, Brideen asked him to
give Barbara his blessing. He gave his
blessing to Brideen herself. She thought
it was to the doll he gave it, and she was
full-satisfied.

Brideen settled a nice little parlour for
Barbara on top of the dresser. She heard
that her Aunt Barbara had a parlour (in
Uachtar Ard she was living), and she thought
that it wasn't too much for Barbara to have
a parlour as good as anybody. My poor
Barbara fell from the top of the dresser one
day, as I have told already, and one of her
legs was broken. It's many a disaster over
that happened her. Another day the dog
grabbed her, and was tearing her joint from

joint till Brideen's mother came to help her.
The one leg remained safe with the dog.
She fell into the river another time, and
she had like to be drowned. It's Brideen's
father that came to her help this journey.
Brideen herself was almost drowned, and
she trying to save her from the river-
bank.

If Barbara wasn't too well-favoured the
first day she came, it stands to nature it's
not better the appearance was on her after
putting a year by her. But 'twas all the
same to Brideen whether she was well-
favoured or ill-favoured. She gave the
love of her heart to her from the first
minute she laid an eye on her, and it's
increasing that love was from day to day.
Isn't it the two of them used to have the
fun when the mother would leave the house
to their care, times she'd be visiting in a
neighbour's house! They would have the
floor swept and the plates washed before
her, when she'd return. And isn't it on
the mother would be the wonder, *mor
'eadh!*

"Is it Brideen cleaned the floor for her
mama?" she'd say.

271

" Brideen and Barbara," the little girl would say.

" *Muise*, I don't know what I'd do, if it weren't for the pair of you !" the mother would say. And isn't it on Brideen would be the delight and the pride !

And the long days of summer they would put from them on the hillside, among the fern and flowers !—Brideen gathering daisies and fairy-thimbles and buttercups, and Barbara reckoning them for her (so she'd say) ; Brideen forever talking and telling tales that a human being (not to say a little doll) never heard the likes of before or since, and Barbara listening to her ; it must be she'd be listening attentively, for there wouldn't come a word out of her mouth.

It's my opinion that there wasn't a little girl in Connacht, or if I might say it, in the Continent of Europe, that was more contented and happy-like, than Brideen was those days ; and, I declare, there wasn't a little doll under the hollow of the sun that was more contented and happy-like than Barbara.

That's how it stood till Niamh Goldy-Head came.

II

Niamh Goldy-Head was a native of Dublin. A lady that came to Gortmore learning Irish promised before leaving that she'd send some valuable to Brideen. And, sure, she did. One day, about a week after her departure, Bartly the Postman walked in into the middle of the kitchen and laid a big box on the floor.

"For you, young woman," says he to Brideen.

"*Ara*, what's in it, Bartly?"

"How do I know? A fairy, maybe."

"*O bhó!* Where did you get it?"

"From a little green maneen, with a long blue beard on him, a red cap on his nob, and he riding a hare."

"*Ora*, daddy! And what did he say to you, Bartly?"

"Devil a thing did he say only, 'Give this to Brideen, and my blessing,' and off with him while you'd be winking."

I am doubtful if this story of Bartly's

273 T

was all true, but Brideen believed every
word of it. She called to her mother, where
she was inside in the room tidying the place
after the breakfast.

" Mama, mama, a big box for Brideen !
A little green maneen, with a long blue
beard on him, that gave it to Bartly the
Postman ! "

The mother came out and Bartly gathered
off.

" Mameen, mameen, open the box quick !
Bartly thinks it's maybe a fairy is in it !
Hurry, mameen, or how do we know he
won't be smothered inside in the box ? "

The mother cut the string. She tore the
paper from the box. She lifted the lid.
What should be in it, lying nice and comfort-
ably in the box, like a child would be in a
cradle, but the grandest and the beautifullest
doll that eye ever saw ! There was yellow-
golden hair on it, and it falling in ringleted
tresses over its breast and over its shoulders.
There was the blush of the rose on its cheek.
It's the likeness I'd compare its little mouth
to—two rowanberries ; and 'twas like pearls
its teeth were. Its eyes were closed. There
was a bright suit of silk covering its body,

274

and a red mantle of satin over that outside.
There was a glittering necklace of noble
stones about its throat, and, as a top on all
the wonders, there was a royal crown on
its head.

"A Queen!" says Brideen in a whisper,
for there was a kind of dread on her before
this glorious fairy. "A Queen from Tir-
na-nOg! Look, mama, she's asleep. Do
you think will she waken?"

"Take her in your hand," says the
mother.

The little girl stretched out her two
hands timidly, laid them reverently on the
wonderful doll, and at last lifted it out of
the box. No sooner did she take it than
the doll opened its eyes, and said in a sweet,
weeny voice:

"Mam—a!"

"God bless us!" says the mother, making the sign of the cross on herself, "she
can talk!"

There was a queer edge in Brideen's
eyes, and there was a queer light in her
features. But I don't think she was half as
scared as the mother was. Children do be
expecting wonders always, and when a

wonderful thing happens it doesn't put as much astonishment on them as it does on grown people.

"Why wouldn't she talk?" says Brideen. "Can't Barbara talk? But it's sweeter entirely this voice than Barbara's voice."

My grief, you are, Barbara! Where were you all this time? Lying on the floor where you fell from Brideen's hand when Bartly came in. I don't know did you hear these words from your friend's mouth. If you did, it's surely they'd go like a stitch through your heart.

Brideen continued speaking. She spoke quickly, her two eyes dancing in her head:

"A Queen this is," says she. "A fairy Queen! Look at the fine suit she's wearing! Look at the mantle of satin is on her! Look at the beautiful crown she has! She's like yon Queen that Stephen of the Stories was discoursing about the other night,—the Queen that came over sea from Tir-na-nOg riding on the white steed. What's the name that was on that Queen, mama?"

"Niamh of the Golden Head.'

"This is Niamh Goldy-Head!" says the

little girl. " I'll show her to Stephen the
first other time he comes ! Isn't it he will
be glad to see her, mama? He was angry
the other night when my daddy said there
are no fairies at all in it. I knew my daddy
was only joking."

I wouldn't like to say that Niamh Goldy-
Head was a fairy, as Brideen thought, but
I'm sure there was some magic to do with
her ; and I'm full-sure that Brideen herself
was under a spell from the moment she
came into the house. If she weren't, she
wouldn't leave Barbara lying by herself on
the floor through the evening, without
saying a word to her, or even remembering
her, till sleep-time ; nor would she go to
sleep without bringing Barbara into the bed
with her, as was her habit. It's with trouble
you'd believe it, but it's the young Queen
that slept along with Brideen that night,
instead of the faithful little companion that
used sleep with her every night for a year.

Barbara remained lying on the floor, till
Brideen's mother found her, and lifted and
put her on top of the dresser where her
own little parlour was. Barbara spent that
night on the top of the dresser. I didn't

hear that Brideen or her mother or her
father noticed any lamenting from the
kitchen in the middle of the night, and, to say
truth, I don't think that Barbara shed a tear.
But it's certain she was sad enough, lying
up yonder by herself, without her friend's
arm about her, without the heat of her
friend's body warming her, without man or
mortal near her, without hearing a sound
but the faint, truly-lonesome sounds that do
be heard in a house in the dead time of the
night.

III

It's sitting or lying on the top of the
dresser that Barbara spent the greater
part of the next quarter. 'Twas seldom
Brideen used speak to her ; and when she
would speak, she'd only say, " Be a good
girl, Barbara. You see I'm busy. I must
give attention to Niamh Goldy-Head. She's
a Queen, you know, and she must be
attended well." Brideen was getting older
now (I believe she was five years past, or,
maybe, five and a-half), and she was rising
out of a share of the habits she learned at
the start of her babyhood. It's not " Brideen " she'd call herself now, for she knew
the meaning that was in the little word
" I," and in those little tails " am " and
"am not" when they're put after "I." She
knew, too, that it's great the respect and
the honour due to a Queen, over what is due
to a poor, little creatureen like Barbara.

I'm afraid Barbara didn't understand this
story at all. She was only a little wooden

doll, and, sure, 'twould be hard for its likes
to understand the heart of a girl. It was
plain to her that she was cast to one
side. It's Niamh Goldy-Head would
sleep along with Brideen now ; it's Niamh
Goldy-Head would sit beside her at
meal-time ; its Niamh Goldy-head would
go out on the hill, foot to foot with
her, that would lie with her among the
fern, and would go with her gathering
daisies and fairy-thimbles. It's Niamh
Goldy-Head she'd press to her breast. It's
Niamh Goldy-Head she'd kiss. Some other
body to be in the place you'd be, some other
body to be walking with the person you'd
walk with, some other body to be kissing
the mouth you'd long to kiss,—that's the
greatest pain is to be suffered in this world ;
and that's the pain was in Barbara's heart
now, torturing her from morning till night,
and tormenting her from night till morning.

I suppose it'll be said to me that it's not
possible for these thoughts, or any other
thoughts, to be in Barbara's heart, for
wasn't she only a wooden toy, without
feeling, without mind, without understanding, without strength ? My answer to

anybody who'd speak like this to me would
be :—*How do we know?* How do you or I
know that dolls, and wooden toys, and the
tree, and the hill, and the river, and the
waterfall, and the little blossoms of the
field, and the little stones of the strand
haven't their own feeling, and mind, and
understanding, and guidance?—aye, and the
hundred other things we see about us? I
don't say they have ; but 'twould be daring for
me or for anybody else to say that they haven't.
The children think they have ; and it's my
opinion that the children are more discerning in things of this sort than you or I.

One day that Barbara was sitting up
lonesomely by herself in her parlour, Brideen
and Niamh Goldy-Head were in earnest
conversation by the fireside ; or, I ought to
say, Brideen was in earnest conversation with
herself, and Niamh listening to her ; for
nobody ever heard a word out of the Queen's
mouth but only "Mam-a." Brideen's mother
was outside the door washing. The father
was setting potatoes in the garden. There
only remained in the house Brideen and the
two dolls.

It's like the little girl was tired, for she'd

spent the morning washing (she'd wash the
Queen's sheet and blanket every week). It
was short till sleep came on her. It was
short, after that, till she dropped her head
on her breast and she was in deep slumber. I
don't rightly understand what happened after
that, but, by all accounts, Brideen was falling
down and down, till she was stretched on
the hearth-flag within the nearness of an
inch to the fire. She didn't waken, for
she was sound asleep. It's like that Niamh
Goldy-Head was asleep, too, but, however, or whatever, the story is, she didn't
stir. There wasn't a soul in the house to pro-
tect the darling little child from the death that
was faring on her. Nobody knew her to be
in peril, but only God and—Barbara.

The mother was working without, and
she not thinking that death was that near the
child of her heart. She was turning a
tune to herself, and lifting it finely, when
she heard a " plop "—a sound as if something was falling on the floor.

" What's that, now ? " says she to herself.
" Something that fell from the wall, it's a
chance. It can't be that Brideen meddled
with it ? "

In with her in a hurry. It's barely the
life didn't drop out of her, with the dint of
fright. And what wonder? Her darling
child was stretched on the hearth, and her
little coateen blazing in the fire!

The mother rushed to her across the
kitchen, lifted her in her arms, and pulled
the coat from her. She only just saved
her. If she'd waited another little. half-
moment, she was too late.

Brideen was awake now, and her two
arms about the neck of her mother. She
was trembling with the dint of fear, and,
sure enough, crying, though it isn't too
well she understood the story yet. Her
mother was " smothering her with kisses
and drowning her with tears."

"What happened me, mama? I was
dreaming. I felt hot, and I thought I was
going up, up in the sky, and that the sun
was burning me? What happened me?"

"It's the will of God that my *stóirín* wasn't
burnt,—not with the sun, but with the fire.
O, Brideen, your mother's little pet, what
would I do if they'd kill you on me?
What would your father do? 'Twas God
spoke to me coming in that minute!—I

don't know what sort of noise I heard? If it weren't for that, I mightn't have come in at all."

She looked round her. Everything was in its own place on the table, and on the walls, and on the dresser,—but stay! In front of the dresser she took notice of a thing on the floor. What was it? A little body without a head—a doll's body.

"Barbara fallen from the dresser again," says the mother. "My conscience, it's she saved your life to you, Brideen."

"Not falling she did it at all!" says the little girl, "but it's how she saw I was in danger, and she threw a leap from the top of the dresser to save me. O, poor Barbara, you gave your life for my sake!"

She went on her knees, lifted the little corpse of the doll, and kissed it softly and fondly.

"Mama," says she, sadly, "since Niamh Goldy-Head came, I'm afraid I forgot poor Barbara, and it's greater the liking I put in Niamh Goldy-Head than in her; and see, it's she was most true to me in the end. And she's dead now on me, and I won't be able to speak with her ever again, nor to say to

284

her that I'd rather her a thousand times,—
aye, a hundred thousand times — than
Niamh."

"It's not dead she is at all," says the
mother, "but hurted. Your father will
put the head on her again when he comes in."

"If I'd fall from the top of the dresser,
mama, and lose my head, would he be able
to put it on me again?"

"He wouldn't. But you're not the same
as Barbara."

"I am the same. She's dead. Don't
you see she's not moving or speaking?"

The mother had to admit this much.

Nothing would convince Brideen that
Barbara wasn't killed, and that it wasn't to
save her she gave her life. I myself wouldn't
say she was right, but I wouldn't say she
wasn't. I can only say what I said before:
How do I know? How do you know?

Barbara was buried that evening on the
side of the hill in the place where she and
Brideen spent those long days of summer
among the fern and the flowers. There
are fairy-thimbles growing at the head of
the grave, and daisies and buttercups plenti-
fully about it.

285

EOINEEN OF THE BIRDS

A conversation that took place between Eoineen of the Birds and his mother, one evening of spring, before the going under of the sun. The song-thrush and the yellow-bunting that heard it, and (as I think) told it to my friends the swallows. The swallows that told the story to me.

"Come on in, pet. It's rising cold."

"I can't stir a while yet, little mother. I'm waiting for the swallows."

"For what, little son?"

"The swallows. I'm thinking they'll be here this night."

Eoineen was high on the big rock that was close to the gable of the house, he settled nicely on top of it, and the white back of his head against the foot of the ash-tree that was sheltering him. He had his head raised, and he looking from him southward. His mother looked up at him. It seemed to her that his share of hair was yellow gold where the sun was burning on his head.

ʊ

" And. where are they coming from, child ? "

" From the Southern World—the place it does be summer always. I'm expecting them for a week."

" And how do you know that it's this night they'll come ? "

"I don't know, only thinking it. 'Twould be time for them to be here some day now. I mind that it was this day surely they came last year. I was coming up from the well when I heard their twittering—a sweet, joyful twittering as they'd be saying : 'We've come to you again, Eoineen ! News to you from the Southern World ! '—and then one of them flew past me, rubbing his wing to my cheek."

There's no need to say that this talk put great wonder on the mother. Eoineen never spoke to her like that before. She knew that he put a great wish in the birds, and that it's many an hour he used spend in the wood or by the strand-side, " talking to them," as he'd say. But she didn't understand why there should be that great a wish on him to see the swallows coming again. She knew by his face, as

well as by the words of his mouth, that he
was forever thinking on some thing that
was making him anxious. And there came
unrest on the woman over it, a thing that's
no wonder. "Sure, it's queer talk from
a child," says she in her own mind. She
didn't speak a breath aloud, however, but
she listening to each word that came out of
his mouth.

"I'm very lonely since they left me in
the harvest," says the little boy again, like
one that would be talking to himself.
"They had that much to say to me.
They're not the same as the song-thrush
or the yellow-bunting that do spend the
best part of their lives by the ditch-side in
the garden. They do have wonderful
stories to tell about the lands where it does
be summer always, and about the wild seas
where the ships are drowned, and about the
lime-bright cities where the kings do be
always living. It's long, long the road
from the Southern World to this country.
They see everything coming over, and they
don't forget anything. I think long, wanting them."

"Come in, white love, and go to sleep.

You'll be perished with the cold if you stay out any longer."

" I'll go in presently, little mother. I wouldn't like them to come, and I not to be here to give them welcome. They would be wondering."

The mother saw that it was no good to be at him. She went in, troubled. She cleaned the table and the chairs. She washed the vessels and the dishes. She took the brush, and she brushed the floor. She scoured the kettle and the big pot. She trimmed the lamp, and hung it on the wall. She put more turf on the fire. She did a hundred other things that she needn't have done. Then she sat before the fire, thinking to herself.

The " piper of the ashes " (the cricket) came out, and started on his heartsome tune. The mother stayed by the hearth-side, pondering. The little boy stayed on his airy seat, watching. The cows came home from the pasture. The hen called to her her chickens. The blackbird and the wren, and the other little people of the wood went to sleep. The buzzing of the flies was stopped, and the bleating of the lambs. The sun sank slowly till it was close to the bottom of the sky, till it was exactly on the bottom of the sky, till it was under the bottom of the sky. A cold wind blew from the east. The darkness spread on the earth. At last Eoineen came in.

"I fear they won't come this night," says he. "Maybe, with God's help, they might come to-morrow."

.   .   .   .

The morning of the next day came. Eoineen was up early, and he watching out from the top of the rock. The middle of day came. The end of day came. The night came. But, my grief! the swallows did not come.

"Maybe we might see them here to-morrow," says Eoineen, and he coming in sadly that night.

But they didn't see them. Nor did they see them the day after that, nor the day after that again. And it's what Eoineen would say every night and he coming in:

"Maybe they might be with us to-morrow."

II

There came a delightful evening in the
end of April. The air was clear and cool
after a shower of rain. There was a wonderful light in the western heavens. The birds
sang a strain of music in the wood. The
waves were chanting a poem on the strand.
But loneliness was on the heart of the boy
and he waiting for the swallows.

There was heard, suddenly, a sound that
hadn't been heard in that place for more
than a half-year. A little, tiny sound. A
faint, truly-melodious sound. A pert, joy-
ous twittering, and it unlike any other
twittering that comes from the mouth of a
bird. With fiery swiftness a small black
body drove from the south. It flying high
in the air. Two broad, strong wings on it.
The shaping of a fork on its tail. It cutting
the way before it, like an arrow shot from a
bow. It swooped suddenly, it turned, rose
again, swooped and turned again. Then it
made straight for Eoineen, it speaking at

the top of its voice, till it lay and nestled in the breast of the little boy after its long journey from the Southern World.

"O, my love, my love you are!" says Eoineen, taking it in his two hands and kissing it on the little black head. "Welcome to me from the strange countries! Are you tired after your lonely journey over lands and over seas? *Ora*, my thousand, thousand loves you are, beautiful little messenger from the country where it does be summer always! Where are your companions from you? Or what happened you on the road, or why didn't ye come before this?"

While he was speaking like this with the swallow, kissing it again and yet again, and rubbing his hand lovingly over its blue-black wings, its little red throat and its bright, feathered breast, another little bird sailed from the south and alighted beside them. The two birds rose in the air then, and it is the first other place they lay, in their own little nest that was hidden in the ivy that was growing thickly on the walls of the house.

"They are found at last, little mother!"

says Eoineen, and he running in joyfully.
" The swallows are found at last ! A pair
came this night—the pair who have their
nest over my window. The others will be
with us to-morrow."

The mother stooped and drew him to
her. Then she put a prayer to God in a
whisper, giving thanks to Him for sending.
the swallows to them. The flame that was
in the eyes of the boy, it would put delight
on the heart of any mother at all.

It was sound the sleep of Eoineen that
night.

.   .   .   .

The swallows came one after another
now—singly at first, in pairs then, and at
last in little flocks. Isn't it they were glad
when they saw the old place again ! The
little wood and the brook running through
it ; the white, sandy beach ; the ash-trees
that were close to the house ; the house
itself and the old nests exactly as they left
them half a year before that. There was no
change on anything but only on the little
boy. He was quieter and gentler than
he used to be. He was oftener sitting than

running with himself about the fields, as
was his habit before that. He wasn't heard
laughing or singing as often as he used be
heard. If the swallows took notice of this
much—and I wouldn't say they didn't—it's
certain that they were sorry for him.

The summer went by. It was seldom
Eoineen would stir out on the street, but he
sitting contentedly on the top of the rock,
looking at the swallows and listening to their
twittering. He'd spend the hours like this.
'Twas often he was there from early morning till there came "*tráthnóna gréine buidhe*,"
—the evening of the yellow sun ; and going
within every night he'd have a great lot of
stories, beautiful, wonderful stories, to tell
to his mother. When she'd question him
about these stories, he'd always say to her
that it's from the swallows he'd get them.

III.

The priest came in the evening.

" How is Eoineen of the Birds this weather, Eibhlin?" says he. (The other boys had nicknamed him " Eoineen of the Birds" on account of the love he had for the birds.)

" *Muise*, Father, he wasn't as well for many a long day as he is since the summer came. There's a blush in his cheek I never saw in it before."

The priest looked sharply at her. He had noticed that blush for a time, and if he did, it didn't deceive him. Other people had noticed it, too, and if they did, it didn't deceive them. But it was plain it deceived the mother. There were tears in the priest's eyes, but Eibhlin was blowing the fire, and she didn't see them. There was a stoppage in his voice when he spoke again, but the mother didn't notice it.

" Where's Eoineen now, Eibhlin?"

" He's sitting on the rock outside, 'talking

298

to the swallows,' as himself says. It's
wonderful the affection he has for those
little birds. Do you know, Father, what
he said to me the other day?"

" I don't know, Eibhlin."

" He was saying that it's short now till
the swallows would be departing from us
again, and says he to me, suddenly, ' What
would you do, little mother,' says he, ' if
I'd steal away from you with the swallows?'"

" And what did you say, Eibhlin?"

" I said to him to brush out with him,
and not be bothering me. But I'm thinking ever since on the thing he said, and it's
troubling me. Wasn't it a queer thought
for him, Father,—he going with the
swallows?"

" It's many a queer thought comes into
the heart of a child," says the priest. And
he went out the door, without saying
another word.

.   .   .   .

" Dreaming, as usual, Eoineen?"

" No, Father. I'm talking to the
swallows."

" Talking to them?"

"Aye, Father. We do be talking together always."

"And whisper. What do ye be saying to one another?"

"We do be talking about the countries far away, where it does be summer always, and about the wild seas where the ships do be drowned, and about the lime-bright cities where the kings do be always living."

The wonder of his heart came on the priest, as it came on the mother before that.

"It's you do be discoursing on these things, and they listening to you, it's like?"

"No, Father. They, mostly, that do be talking, and I listening to them."

"And do you understand their share of talk, Eoineen?"

"Aye, Father. Don't you understand it?"

"Not too well I understand it. Make room for me on the rock there, and I'll sit a while till ,you explain to me what they do be saying."

Up with the priest on the rock, and he sat beside the little boy. He put an arm about his neck, and began taking talk out of him.

" Tell me what the swallows do be saying to you, Eoineen."

" It's many a thing they do be saying to me. It's many a fine story they do tell to me. Did you see that little bird that went past just now, Father ? "

" I did."

" That's the cleverest storyteller of them all. That one's nest is under the ivy that's growing over the window of my room. And she has another nest in the Southern World—herself and her mate."

" Has she, Eoineen ? "

" Aye — another beautiful little nest thousands and thousands of miles from this. Isn't it a queer story, Father ?—to say that the little swallow has two houses, and we having one only ? "

" It's queer, indeed. And what sort is the country she has this other house in ? "

" When I shut my eyes I see a lonely, awful country. I see it now, Father ! A lonely, terrible country. There's neither mountain, nor hill, nor valley in it, but it a great, level, sandy plain. There's neither wood, nor grass, nor growth in it, but the earth as bare as the heart of your palm.

Sand entirely. Sand under your feet. Sand
on every side of you. The sun scorching
over your head. Without a cloud at all
to be seen in the sky. It very h t. H e
and tn re there's a little grassy spot, as it
would be a little island in the middle of the
sea. A couple of high trees growing on
each spot of them. They sheltered from
wind and sun. I see on one of these islands
a high cliff. A terrible big cliff. There's
a cleft in the cliff, and in the cleft there's
a little swallow's nest. That's the nest of
my little swallow."

"Who told you this, Eoineen?"

"The swallow. She spends half of her
life in that country, herself and her mate.
Isn't it the grand life they have on that
lonely little island in the middle of the
desert! There does be neither cold nor
wet in it, frost nor snow, but it summer
always. . . . And after that, Father, they
don't forget their other little nest here in
Ireland, nor the wood, nor the brook, nor
the ash-trees, nor me, nor my mother. Every
year in the spring they hear, as it would be, a
whispering in their ears telling them that
the woods are in leaf in Ireland, and that

302

the sun is shining on the bawn-fields, and
that the lambs are bleating, and I waiting
for them. And they bid farewell to their
dwelling in the strange country, and they
go before them, and they make neither stop
nor stay till they see the tops of the ash-trees
from them, and till they hear the voice of
the river and the bleating of the lambs."

The priest was listening attentively.

" O !—and isn't it wonderful the journey
they do have from the Southern World !
They leave the big sandy plain behind them,
and the high, bald mountains that are on
its border, and they go before them till they
come to the great sea. Out with them
over the sea, flying always, always, without
weariness, without growing weak. They
see below them the mighty-swelling waves,
and the ships ploughing the ocean, and
the white sails, and seagulls, and the ' black
hags of the sea ' (cormorants), and other
wonders that I couldn't remember. And
times, there rise wind and storm, and they
see the ships drowning and the waves rising
on top of each other ; and themselves, the
creatures, do be beaten with the wind, and
blinded with the rain and with the salt water,

IV

August and September went. October was half out. As the days were getting shorter, Eoineen was rising sadder. 'Twas seldom he'd speak to his mother now, but every night before going to sleep he'd kiss her fondly and tenderly, and he'd say:

"Call me early in the morning, little mother. It's little time I have now. They'll be departing without much delay."

A beautiful day brightened in the middle of the month. Early in the morning, Eoineen took notice that the swallows were crowding together on the top of the house. He didn't stir from his seat the length of that day. Coming in in the evening, says he to his mother:

"They'll be departing to-morrow."

"How do you know, white love?"

"They told me to-day. . . . Little mother," says he again, after a spell of silence.

"What is it, little child?"

"I can't stay here when they're gone. I

305

must go along with them. . . . to the
country where it does be summer always.
You wouldn't be lonely if I'd go?"

"O! treasure, my thousand treasures,
don't speak to me like that!" says the
mother, taking him and squeezing him to
her heart. "You're not to be stolen from
me! Sure, you wouldn't leave your little
mother, and go after the swallows?"

Eoineen didn't say a word, but to kiss her
again and again.

. . . . . .

Another day brightened. The little, wee
boy was up early. From the start of day
hundreds of swallows were gathered together
on the ridge of the house. From time to
time one or two of them would go off and
they'd return again, as if they'd be considering the weather. At last a pair went off
and they didn't return. Another pair went
off. The third pair went. They were
going one after another then, till there didn't
remain but one little flock only on the horn
of the house. The pair that came first on
yon evening of spring six months before that
were in this little flock. It's like they were
loath to leave the place.

EOINEEN OF THE BIRDS

Eoineen was watching them from the rock. His mother was standing beside him.

The little flock of birds rose in the air, and they faced the Southern World. Going over the top of the wood a pair turned back,—the pair whose nest was over the window. Down with them from the sky, making on Eoineen. Over with them then, they flying close to the ground. Their wings rubbed a cheek of the little boy, and they sweeping past him. Up with them in the air again, they speaking sorrowfully, and off for ever with them after the other crowd.

"Mother," says Eoineen, "they're calling me. 'Come to the country where the sun does be shining always,—come, Eoineen, over the wild seas to the Country of Light, — come, Eoineen of the Birds!' I can't deny them. A blessing with you, little mother,—my thousand, thousand blessings to you, little mother of my heart. I'm going from you . . . over the wild seas . . . to the country where it does be summer always."

He let his head back on his mother's shoulder and he put a sigh out of him.

307

There was heard the crying of a woman in that lonely place—the crying of a mother keening her child. Eoineen was departed along with the swallows.

. . . . . .

Autumn and winter went by and the spring was at hand again. The woods were in leaf, and the lambs bleating, and the sun shining on the bawn-fields. One glorious evening in April the swallows came. There was a wonderful light at the bottom of the sky in the west, as it was a year from that time. The birds sang a strain of music in the wood. The waves chanted a poem on the strand. But there was no little white-haired boy, sitting on the top of the rock under the shadow of the ash-trees. Inside in the house there was a solitary woman, weeping by the fire.

" . . . And, darling little son," says she, " I see the swallows here again, but I'll never, never see you here."

The swallows heard her, and they going past the door. I don't know did Eoineen hear her, as he was thousands of miles away . . . in the country where it does be summer always.

308

LULLABY OF A WOMAN OF THE MOUNTAIN

Little gold head, my house's candle,
You will guide all wayfarers that walk this
  mountain.

Little soft mouth that my breast has known,
Mary will kiss you as she passes.

Little round cheek, O smoother than satin,
Jesus will lay His hand on you.

Mary's kiss on my baby's mouth,
Christ's little hand on my darling's cheek!

House, be still, and ye little grey mice,
Lie close to-night in your hidden lairs.

Moths on the window, fold your wings,
Little black chafers, silence your humming.

Plover and curlew, fly not over my house,
Do not speak, wild barnacle, passing over
  this mountain.

Things of the mountain that wake in the
  night-time,
Do not stir to-night till the daylight
  whitens!

A WOMAN OF THE MOUNTAIN
KEENS HER SON

Grief on the death, it has blackened my
 heart :
It has snatched my love and left me desolate,
Without friend or companion under the
 roof of my house
But this sorrow in the midst of me, and I
 keening.

As I walked the mountain in the evening
The birds spoke to me sorrowfully,
The sweet snipe spoke and the voiceful
 curlew
Relating to me that my darling was dead.

I called to you and your voice I heard not,
I called again and I got no answer,
I kissed your mouth, and O God how cold
 it was !
Ah, cold is your bed in the lonely churchyard.

O green-sodded grave in which my child is,
Little narrow grave, since you are his bed,

WHY DO YE TORTURE ME?

Why are ye torturing me, O desires of my
    heart?
Torturing me and paining me by day and
    by night?
Hunting me as a poor deer would be hunted
    on a hill,
A poor long-wearied deer with the hound-
    pack after him?

There's no ease to my paining in the loneli-
    ness of the hills,
But the cry of the hunters terrifically to be
    heard,
The cry of my desires haunting me without
    respite,—
O ravening hounds, long is your run!

No satisfying can come to my desires while
    I live,
For the satisfaction I desired yesterday is no
    satisfaction,
And the hound-pack is the greedier of the
    satisfaction it has got,—
And forever I shall not sleep till I sleep in
    the grave.

A SONG FOR MARY MAGDALENE

O woman of the gleaming hair,
(Wild hair that won men's gaze to thee)
Weary thou turnest from the common
    stare,
For the *shuiler* Christ is calling thee.

O woman of the snowy side,
Many a lover hath lain with thee,
Yet left thee sad at the morning tide,
But thy lover Christ shall comfort thee.

O woman with the wild thing's heart,
Old sin hath set a snare for thee :
In the forest ways forspent thou art
But the hunter Christ shall pity thee.

O woman spendthrift of thyself,
Spendthrift of all the love in thee,
Sold unto sin for little pelf,
The captain Christ shall ransom thee.

O woman that no lover's kiss
(Tho' many a kiss was given thee)
Could slake thy love, is it not for this
The hero Christ shall die for thee ?

ON THE STRAND OF
HOWTH

On the strand of Howth
Breaks a sounding wave;
A lone sea-gull screams
Above the bay.

In the middle of the meadow
Beside Glasnevin
The corncrake speaks
All night long.

There is minstrelsy of birds
In Glenasmole,
The blackbird and thrush
Chanting music.

There is shining of sun
On the side of Slieverua,
And the wind blowing
Down over its brow.

On the harbour of Dunleary
Are boat and ship
With sails set
Ploughing the waves.

THE DORD FEINNE

'Se do bheatha, O woman that wast sorrowful,
What grieved us was thy being in chains,
Thy beautiful country in the possession of
rogues,
> And thou sold to the Galls,
> *Oró, 'se do bheatha a bhaile,*
> *Oró, 'se do bheatha a bhaile,*
> *Oró, 'se do bheatha a bhaile,*
> Now at summer's coming !

Thanks to the God of miracles that we see,
Altho' we live not a week thereafter,
Gráinne Mhaol and a thousand heroes
> Proclaiming the scattering of the Galls !
> *Oró, 'se do bheatha a bhaile,*
> *Oró, 'se do bheatha a bhaile,*
> *Oró, 'se do bheatha a bhaile,*
> Now at summer's coming !

Gráinne Mhaol is coming from over the sea,
The Fenians of Fál as a guard about her,
Gaels they, and neither French nor Spaniard,
> And a rout upon the Galls !
> *Oró, 'se do bheatha a bhaile,*
> *Oró, 'se do bheatha a bhaile,*
> *Oró, 'se do bheatha a bhaile,*
> Now at summer's coming !

THE MOTHER

I do not grudge them : Lord, I do not grudge
My two strong sons that I have seen go out
To break their strength and die, they and
    a few,
In bloody protest for a glorious thing,
They shall be spoken of among their people,
The generations shall remember them,
And call them blessed ;
But I will speak their names to my own heart
In the long nights ;
The little names that were familiar once
Round my dead hearth.
Lord, thou art hard on mothers :
We suffer in their coming and their going ;
And tho' I grudge them not, I weary, weary
Of the long sorrow—And yet I have my joy :
My sons were faithful, and they fought.

THE FOOL

Since the wise men have not spoken, I speak
    that am only a fool ;
A fool that hath loved his folly,
Yea, more than the wise men their books or
    their counting houses, or their quiet
    homes,
Or their fame in men's mouths ;
A fool that in all his days hath done never
    a prudent thing,
Never hath counted the cost, nor recked if
    another reaped
The fruit of his mighty sowing, content
    to scatter the seed ;
A fool that is unrepentant, and that soon at
    the end of all
Shall laugh in his lonely heart as the ripe
    ears fall to the reaping-hooks
And the poor are filled that were empty,
Tho' he go hungry.

I have squandered the splendid years that
    the Lord God gave to my youth
In attempting impossible things, deeming
    them alone worth the toil.

THE FOOL

Was it folly or grace? Not men shall
    iudge me, but God.

I have squandered the splendid years:
Lord, if I had the years I would squander
    them over again,
Aye, fling them from me !
For this I have heard in my heart, that a
    man shall scatter, not hoard,
Shall do the deed of to-day, nor take thought
    of to-morrow's teen,
Shall not bargain or huxter with God ; or
    was it a jest of Christ's
And is this my sin before men, to have
    taken Him at His word ?

The lawyers have sat in council, the men
    with the keen, long faces,
And said, " This man is a fool," and others
    have said, " He blasphemeth ;"
And the wise have pitied the fool that hath
    striven to give a life
In the world of time and space among the
    bulks of actual things,
To a dream that was dreamed in the heart,
    and that only the heart could hold.

THE FOOL

O wise men, riddle me this: what if the
    dream come true ?
What if the dream come true ? and if
    millions unborn shall dwell
In the house that I shaped in my heart, the
    noble house of my thought ?
Lord, I have staked my soul, I have staked
    the lives of my kin
On the truth of Thy dreadful word. Do
    not remember my failures,
But remember this my faith.

And so I speak.
Yea, ere my hot youth pass, I speak to my
    people and say :
Ye shall be foolish as I ; ye shall scatter,
    not save ;
Ye shall venture your all, lest ye lose what
    is more than all ;
Ye shall call for a miracle, taking Christ at
    His word.
And for this I will answer, O people, answer
    here and hereafter,
O people that I have loved shall we not
    answer together ?

THE REBEL

I am come of the seed of the people, the
      people that sorrow,
That have no treasure but hope,
No riches laid up but a memory
Of an Ancient glory.
My mother bore me in bondage, in bondage
      my mother was born,
I am of the blood of serfs;
The children with whom I have played, the
      men and women with whom I have
      eaten,
Have had masters over them, have been
      under the lash of masters,
And, though gentle, have served churls;
The hands that have touched mine, the dear
      hands whose touch is familiar to me,
Have worn shameful manacles, have been
      bitten at the wrist by manacles,
Have grown hard with the manacles and the
      task-work of strangers,
I am flesh of the flesh of these lowly, I am
      bone of their bone,
I that have never submitted;
I that have a soul greater than the souls of
      my people's masters,

THE REBEL

I that have vision and prophecy and the gift
    of fiery speech,
I that have spoken with God on the top of
    His holy hill.

And because I am of the people, I understand
    the people,
I am sorrowful with their sorrow, I am
    hungry with their desire:
My heart has been heavy with the grief of
    mothers,
My eyes have been wet with the tears of
    children,
I have yearned with old wistful men,
And laughed or cursed with young men;
Their shame is my shame, and I have
    reddened for it,
Reddened for that they have served, they
    who should be free,
Reddened for that they have gone in want,
    while others have been full,
Reddened for that they have walked in fear
    of lawyers and of their jailors
With their writs of summons and their
    handcuffs,
Men mean and cruel!

THE REBEL

I could have borne stripes on my body
    rather than this shame of my people.

And now I speak, being full of vision;
I speak to my people, and I speak in my
    people's name to the masters of my people.
I say to my people that they are holy, that
    they are august, despite their chains,
That they are greater than those that hold
    them, and stronger and purer,
That they have but need of courage, and to
    call on the name of their God,
God the unforgetting, the dear God that
    loves the peoples
For whom He died naked, suffering shame.
And I say to my people's masters : Beware,
Beware of the thing that is coming, beware
    of the risen people,
Who shall take what ye would not give.
    Did ye think to conquer the people,
Or that Law is stronger than life and than
    men's desire to be free?
We will try it out with you, ye that have
    harried and held,
Ye that have bullied and bribed, tyrants,
    hypocrites, liars !

THE WAYFARER

The beauty of the world hath made me sad,
This beauty that will pass ;
Sometimes my heart hath shaken with great
    joy
To see a leaping squirrel in a tree,
Or a red lady-bird upon a stalk,
Or little rabbits in a field at evening,
Lit by a slanting sun,
Or some green hill where shadows drifted by
Some quiet hill where mountainy man hath
    sown
And soon would reap; near to the gate of
    Heaven;
Or children with bare feet upon the sands
Of some ebbed sea, or playing on the streets
Of little towns in Connacht,
Things young and happy.
And then my heart hath told me :
These will pass,
Will pass and change, will die and be no
    more,
Things bright and green, things young and
    happy ;
And I have gone upon my way
Sorrowful.

APPENDIX

THE SINGER

The following is the version of a passage in this play, which was with the Author's manuscript :

COLM. Is it to die like rats you'd have us because the the word is not given?

CUIMIN. Our plans are not finished. Our orders are not here.

COLM. Our plans will never be finished. Our orders may never be here.

CUIMIN. We've no one to lead us.

COLM. Didn't you elect me your captain?

CUIMIN. We did, but not to bid us rise out when the whole country is quiet. We were to get the word from the men that are over the people. They'll speak when the time comes. (*The door opens again and Feichin comes in with two or three others.*) Am I speaking lie or truth, men? Colm here wants us to rise out before the word comes. I say we must wait for the word. What do do you say, Feichin, you that's got a wiser head than these young fellows?

FEICHIN. God forgive me if I'm wrong, but I say we should wait for our orders.

CUIMIN. What do you say, Diarmaid?

DIARMAID. I like you, Colm, for the way you spoke so well and bravely; but I'm slow to give my voice to

iii

send out the boys of th\` mountain—our poor little handful—to stand with their poor little pikes against the big guns of the Gall. If we had news that they were rising in the other countrysides; but we've got no news.

COLM. Master, you haven't spoken yet. I'm afraid to ask you to speak.

MAOILSHEACHLAINN. Cuimin is right when he says that we must not rise out until we get the word; but what do you say, neighbours, if the man that'll give the word is under the roof of this house?

DIARMAID. What do you mean?

MAOILSHEACHLAINN (*going to the door of the room and throwing it open*). Let you rise out, MacDara, and reveal yourself to the men that are waiting your word!

FEICHIN. Has MacDara come home?

MacDara comes out of the room, Maire ni Fhiannachta and Sighle stand behind him in the doorway.

DIARMAID (*starting up*). That is the man that stood among the people in the fair of Uachtar Ard! (*He goes up to MacDara and kisses his hand.*) I could not get near you yesterday, MacDara, the crowds were so great. What was on me that I didn't know you? Sure I ought to have known that sad, proud head. Maire, men and women yet unborn will bless the pains of your first childing.

MAIRE (*comes forward and takes her son's hand and kisses it*). Soft hand that played at my breast, strong hand that will fall heavy on the Gall, brave hand that will break the yoke! Men of the mountain, my son, MacDara, is the Singer that has quickened the dead years and the young blood. Let the horsemen that sleep in Aileach rise up to-day and follow him into the war!

They come forward, one by one, and kiss his hand.
Colm and Sighle last.

COLM. The Gall have marched from Clifden,

MacDara. I wanted to rise out to-day, but these old men think it is not yet time.

Cuimin. We were waiting for the word.

MacDara. And must I speak the word? Old men, you have left me no choice. I had hoped that more would not be asked of me than to sow the secret word of hope, and that the toil of the reaping would be for others. But I see that one does not serve

IOSAGAN

Author's Foreword to *Iosagán agus Sgealta eile*, which is here translated by Mr. Joseph Campbell :

Putting these stories in order, it is no wonder that my thoughts are on the friends that told them to me, and on the lonely place on the edge of Ireland where they live. I see before my eyes a countryside, hilly, crossed with glens, full of rivers, brimming with lakes ; great horns threatening their tops on the verge of the sky in the north-west ; a narrow, moaning bay stretching in from the sea on each side of a "ross ;" the "ross" rising up from the round of the bay, but with no height compared with the nigh-hand hills or the horns far off; a little cluster of houses in each little glen and mountain gap, and a solitary cabin here and there on the shoulder of the hills. I think I hear the ground-bass of the water-falls and rivers, the sweet cry of the golden plover and curlew, and the low voice of the people in talk by the fireside. . . . My blessing with you little book, to Rossnageeragh and to them in it, my friends !

It is from the "*patairidhe beaga*," the "little soft young things" that Old Matthias used see making sport to themselves on the green that I heard the greater part of the first story. They do be there always, every sunny evening and every fine Sunday morning, running and throwing leaps exactly as they would be when Old Matthias would sit looking on them. I never saw Iosagan among them, but it's like He does be there, for all that. Isn't His wish to be rejoicing on the earth, and isn't His delight to be along with His Father's children? . . . I have told in the story itself the place and the time I heard THE PRIEST. It's well I remember Nora's little house, and the kindly little woman herself, and the three children. Paraig is serving Mass now, and I hear Taimeen has "*Fromsó Framsó*," by heart. . . . It was from Brideen herself that I heard the adventures of Barbara. One evening that we went in on Oilean ni Raithnighe (the Ferny Island), I and she, it was she told it to me, and we sitting on the brink of the lake looking over on the Big Rock. She showed me Barbara's grave the same evening after our coming home, and she took a promise from me that I'd say a prayer for her friend's soul every night of my life. Brideen will be going to school next year, and she will be able to read the story of Barbara out of this, I hope she will like it. . . . As for EOINEEN OF THE BIRDS, I don't know who it was I heard it from, unless it was from the swallows themselves. Yes, I think it was they told it to me one evening that I was stretched in the heather looking at them flying here and there over Loch Eireamhlach. From what mouth the swallows heard the start of the story, I don't know. From the song-thrush and from that yellow-bunting that have their nests in a ditch of the garden, it's like.

To you, sweet friends, people of the telling of my stories, both little and big, I give and dedicate this little book.

CHRONOLOGICAL NOTE

THE SINGER was written in the late Autumn of 1915. Joseph Plunkett was profoundly impressed when he read it. "If Pearse were dead," he said, "this would cause a sensation." Mr. Pearse rather deprecated his view that the play was entirely a personal revelation. No Irish MS. is extant. The two poems THE REBEL and THE FOOL also belong to the same period, and are in no sense translations. The same may be said of ON THE STRAND OF HOWTH and THE MOTHER. With the exceptions of SONG FOR MARY MAGDALENE, RANN OF THE LITTLE PLAYMATE (both taken from THE MASTER), CHRIST'S COMING, CHRISTMAS 1915, DORD FEINNE, and the WAYFARER (written in Kilmainham Jail, May, 1916), the remaining Poems are translations of *Suantraide agus Goltraide* (1914). These twelve poems, DORD FEINNE, and CHRIST'S COMING, are the only poems in this volume originally written in Irish.

THE KING was first produced as an open air play upon the banks of the river which runs through the Hermitage, Rathfarnham, by the students of St. Enda's College. In reference to its subsequent production at the Abbey Theatre, Dublin, 17th May, 1913, Mr. Pearse wrote in *An Macaomh*, Vol. II., No. 2, 1913 : "The play we decided to produce along with THE POST OFFICE, was my morality *An Rí.*" We had enacted it during the previous summer with much pageantry of horses and marchings, at a place in our grounds where an old castellated bridge, not unlike an

APPENDIX

entrance to a monastery, is thrown across a stream, Since that performance I had added some speeches with the object of slightly deepening the characterization." William Pearse played the Abbot's part.

THE MASTER was produced Whitsuntide, 1915, at the Irish Theatre, Hardwicke Street, Dublin, with William Pearse as Ciaran. No Irish MS. is extant. *Iosagán*, the dramatization of the author's story of the same name, was first acted in Cullenswood House, Rathmines, Dublin, in February, 1910, by St. Enda students. Mr. Pearse writes in *An Macaomh*, Vol. I., No. 2, 1909 : "In *Iosagán* I have religiously followed the phraseology of the children and old men in *Iar-Connacht* from whom I have learned the Irish I speak. I have put no word, no speech into the mouths of my little boys which the real little boys of the parish I have in mind—boys whom I know as well as I know my pupils in *Sgoil Eanna*—would not use in the same circumstances. I have given their daily conversation, anglicism, vulgarisms and all ; if I gave anything else my picture would be a false one. *Iosagán* is not a play for ordinary theatres or for ordinary players. It requires a certain atmosphere and a certain attitude of mind on the part of the actors. It has in fact been written for performance in a particular place and by particular players. I know that in that place and by those players it will be treated with the reverence due to a prayer."

The first six stories here given are translations of *An Mátair* (1916). The last four stories are translations of *Iosagán agus Sgéalta eile*, some of which were published in *An Claideam Soluis* in 1905-6, re-published a few years later in book-form.

D. R.

LaVergne, TN USA
22 October 2009
161708LV00001B/62/A